HOW TO
BE A
DISNEY
ADULT

STEINER STORIES

For Imogen, Beth & Jamie.

You are the magic.

"You're dead if you aim only for kids.
Adults are only kids grown up, anyway."

Walt Disney

Contents

Foreword

Usually, I hate forewords. I open the book, see one, and I'm there like, what the fuck have they got to say before they've even got to the introduction? So I apologise for this, but this has become a matter of life or death. Because as much as I love Disney, they also scare the absolute shit out of me.

I've done a lot of research into this book, especially regarding legally releasing it. Annoyingly, it isn't straightforward, and there's more red when it comes to Disney copyright than the room in 50 Shades of Grey. I became so petrified of saying the wrong thing that, at one point, I actually thought Mickey Mouse was going to come after me himself and waterboard me for days on end. Which now I think about it, actually sounds kinda hot.

But we all know that Disney is not a company to be fucked with. And rightly so. Too many people have worked too damn hard that it shouldn't just be a free for all. Not that this stops me from buying 'Disney-inspired' ears from Etsy, but in the grand scheme of things, that is definitely not the most offensive thing I have ever purchased from the internet.

So I declare here, not only in good faith but in fear for my life, that I am not, nor is this book affiliated with the Disney company in any way, shape or form. I am only exercising my freedom of speech to discuss Disney and occasionally make poorly-timed sex jokes.

One day the Disney company will realise they need to hire me, and until that day, if I'm not blacklisted first, I am out here with my Mickey Ears and Joffrey iced coffee all on my own. Anyway, now that bureaucratic shite is over, let's get this show on the road.

Introduction: Why the fuck has this weirdo made us buy her book?

For me, it happened a couple of years ago. I'd thought a lot about this moment throughout the years, but no more so than the weeks that built up to it. They were clearly scared, but what parents aren't when their daughter asks them to sit down for a serious conversation?

'I have to tell you something.' I admitted to them. There was a fear in my mum's eyes I had never seen before; her mind had been running through every Eastenders' duff duff since 1985.

'You're not pregnant, are you?' my Dad asked. If only it were that simple. 'Of course not; she can't be,' my mum quickly responded. I was sitting there shaking, worried about how they were going to take this, when I suddenly realised, 'Wait, what do you mean I can't be...?'

Mum and Dad exchanged awkward looks. 'I just mean...' Mum went on to say. 'You know you have to actually get with a man to get pregnant.' What in the fucking fuck? But she has done me there.

'Can we get back to the point?' I asked them. 'Is that why we're here?' Mum asked. 'Because it isn't men you're interested in?' She sounded more hopeful than when I told her I'd been accepted into university.

'I'm not a lesbian.' If eye roll was a tone of voice, that was exactly how I sounded. 'I was going to say Lydia' Mum loves to use my name in a sentence, even though it could not be more evident she is speaking to me, 'this is all very theatrical for you to just say you're gay.'

'No, this is serious.' I love a good drama, but this wasn't the time for it. 'I need to be honest with you both; if I don't say it now, then maybe I never will.'

I'd promised myself I wouldn't get emotional, but I was losing the battle.

'You can tell us anything.' My Dad reminded me. He was going to regret saying that.

'I know this isn't what you want to hear,' I took a moment to look away and compose myself. 'I just want you to promise me that no matter what happens here, you'll still love me; I'll still be your daughter.'

They nodded in agreement. But even then, I knew there was hesitation.

'I'm a...'

They were sinking back into their chairs.

'a...'

They've been divorced for a decade, but I think they very nearly held hands.

'I'm a Disney Adult.'

Gasps, screeches, tears.

They tried to reassure me, but I'm sure I recall hearing the words 'conversion therapy'. And that was the very last time I spoke to my parents...

I'm kidding, of course. They think I'm a total fucking weirdo, but my parents love me very much. And yet, even in this modern world, Disney Adults are regularly being faced with this kind of aversion. To the point, there are people out there who act like they would rather be diagnosed with a terminal illness than an adult relative who loves Disney.

So, what is a Disney Adult? And why are people more concerned with this than 11-year-olds vaping?

The term was coined a few years ago, even landing itself a spot on Urban Dictionary. However, Disney Adults really got their rise to fame in 2022 when a bride broke mainstream media. She chose to pay for Mickey & Minnie to attend her wedding instead of feeding her guests. This caused some serious controversy online, and I'm not even exaggerating; I've seen people react more calmly to children dying in war zones than this.

I can see why this seems a little far-fetched. But I'm telling you straight up that I'm not only chucking my slice of wedding cake but also the single Father of the Bride I've been flirting with since the ceremony (I've got to pay for Disney World somehow); if Mickey & Minnie walk into a wedding reception. And that, my Disney-loving friends, is precisely what makes me a Disney Adult.

Now, suppose you catch me in the smoking area after an offensive amount of 2-for-1 cocktails on any given Saturday night. In that case, I will argue this topic as if I were in the United Nations General Debate. I will get so wound up, borderline tearful, when people try to tear down Disney Adults.

Yet I've reflected on this scenario many morning afters, all whilst picking fake lashes out of my hair. And I can see why the woman throwing her Pornstar Martini around under the outdoor heaters, screaming about how a fictional mouse has changed her life, may come across as a little bit frightening.

Ever since, I have started to see the humour in the term 'Disney Adult.' How we're so quick to defend ourselves against the people who are genuinely terrified of those who get a kick out of wearing Mickey Ears. And they think we're the losers?

But it doesn't stop there. And it really doesn't. Shortly after the Disney Bride incident, the Internet properly turned on Disney Adults in the way that the Internet likes to turn on anyone. It got to the point where Rolling Stones released an article discussing how Disney Adults became 'the most hated group on the internet', which must've been a massive disappointment to the Neo-Nazis of the world.

Before we get into it, let's look at how a Disney Adult is defined. Urban Dictionary has it down as 'A millennial adult, with or without kids, that can't stop talking about Disney, including the movies or the parks'. I can relate to that, it feels pretty accurate. It then goes on to state, 'One of the most terrifyingly intense people you'll ever encounter.' *Sips vodka and coke out of Mickey Mouse Tumbler* shit, I suppose that does too.

Disney Adults even have their own Wikipedia page, which I dare say doesn't mean anything. We all know we can't factually trust that site; my failed GCSE in history corroborates. But here, there is somewhat more kindness initially, referring to us as 'an adult who is a devout fan of The Walt Disney Company'—end of kindness. We've then got words being thrown around like 'religious cult', 'a plague upon society' and 'they will be the end of Western civilisation'. Which is honestly quite complimentary compared to some of the things I've been called before, especially by my old history teacher.

So why has the world turned on Disney lovers with such spite? Well, the incident a couple of years ago meant a wealth of Disney-related cases suddenly came to light. This gave the world the chance to cast their very much unwanted opinions.

Videos began surfacing of Disney Park guests reacting to seeing the castle reveal, which invoked a completely understandable emotional response. Then, of course, since the world can't stand anyone presenting any kind of positive emotion, they immediately started attacking those people.

Just a few years before this, the Internet exploded over a woman who claimed that Disney World wasn't for childless millennials and they should be banned from the park. This is very relatable to me as a childless 27-year-old teenager who would cause a whole different kind of scene on a Saturday night if she was banned from Disney.

The woman went on a very long-winded and highly entertaining rant about how adults steal the magic from the children and make the lines too long. I can completely agree with this and have come up with a fantastic solution. Instead of child swap, we should do child drop. Think how short the queues would be if all the children were just dropped off somewhere. And if it's magic that they want, then all they have to do is look at the wait times and watch them disappear.

Joking aside, I'm a big fan of kids visiting Disney World. I will talk a lot about Disney magic for children in this book. But for now, they can fuck off out of the France Pavilion and let me enjoy my Grand Marnier Orange Slush in peace.

I know the idea of people enjoying themselves watching movies or at a theme park is scary. I know that being passionate about something or being, it's okay I'm going to say it: happy, is terrifying. Not to mention eating food in the shape of three circles. AH! But I promise we're not trying to change the world into some dystopian future run by princesses or magic. Not yet, anyway.

For me, I swore my allegiance to Walt Disney a long time ago.

It started with the films as a child and a few trips to Orlando. Then, without even realising it, I was going into my teenage years with the Phil Collins Tarzan soundtrack on repeat. Man, he did not have to go so hard on that one.

It took me 6 Walt Disney World 'once in a lifetime' trips before accepting that a house deposit and a mortgage were totally off the cards. Don't get me wrong, I've tried cheaper addictions, like heroin. But I just don't get the same buzz. And quite honestly, the wait for the new theme park rides is much shorter than the wait for any psychiatric help from the NHS. So, Disney was going to have to do it for me. And it does, it really does.

If you're wondering whether you're a Disney Adult, don't worry—this book will answer all your questions. Maybe you're looking to transition from being an ordinary fan to having an all-consuming obsession. If that's the case, pull up a pew and read on because we're about to become best friends.

So, whether you're here for information, a laugh, or exposure therapy, I've got it all for you. Because here you leave today and enter the world of yesterday, tomorrow, and... Well, you know the rest.

Reasons you should read this book

1. It's all about Disney!!!
2. I might make you laugh. Might.
3. It's a comfort blanket against all the Disney Adult hate.
4. You might learn something. Don't have too high expectations though.
5. There are random lists like this throughout the book that are either going to make you love me or hate me. Either way, bring it on.
6. It dives into ALL areas of Disney.
7. You're gonna find it hella relatable.
8. I need the money from this book to feed my addiction.
9. To be fair, I don't really care because you've already bought the book, so don't bother reading it if you can't be arsed. I still get paid.
10. I make Disney sex references.

Step 1: Know the History of Disney*

*not from Wikipedia... Well, not entirely.

If the Mickey Ears and full Disney attire don't give away a Disney Adult, then all you have to do is ask them a question about Disney's history. They will arrogantly launch an answer at you within seconds. I can't tell you shit about world history, but you want to know the backstory of The Haunted Mansion and why there is a ring in the concrete? I'm your girl.

I hate watching quiz shows because it means I quickly realise how little general knowledge I have—and trust me, it's little. But as soon as Janette Manrara took the chair on Celebrity Mastermind to answer questions on the Disney Renaissance era, I was in my element.

Indeed, the sheer wealth of Disney facts I have ingrained into my brain is unlikely to aid me at all in my general life. They cloud so many childhood memories that should I ever find myself on fire, I'm more likely to start singing 'I See the Light' instead of remembering to stop, drop, and roll. Then again, if **that's** how I'm going to go, I can live with that.

Well, I won't, but you know what I mean.

It is my opinion that you can never know too much about something. No, I take that back. I've played a game of Never

Have I Ever with my mum before, and never have I ever quite recovered. But when it comes to specialist subjects, there is no harm in being knowledgeable. It's a shame I didn't have that attitude when I was at university, but it's better late than never.

This means when I'm at Disney World, I'm the one in the queue for Thunder Mountain, explaining the storyline behind the whole ride. Some people find this interesting, and other people just want to play Eye Spy.

Whether you find a Disney know-it-all like me irritating or not, it is an essential part of being a Disney Adult. Because when someone challenges you, which they will, you've got to be ready with the facts. So, if you're not sure about Disney's history, let me take you on a whistle-stop tour of the last century.

For decades, Disney has been a household name. Even during Walt's earliest years, he was beyond famous for the work that he created. Though we may not have been alive then to see it, those works are just as popular now. Just recently, in 2023, we celebrated the Disney company's 100th year. This makes it not only one of the most successful studios in the world but also one of the longest-running.

Walt Disney began animating in 1923 and continued with great success for the decades that followed. 1937 saw Walt's (and the world's) first feature-length film debut, and Snow White soon became the highest-grossing film of that time.

This was only the beginning of his movies. We know all too well there was a shit ton more to come. What many aren't aware of is that Walt's story starts long before Snow White, even before any of his films.

Born in 1901 to Elias and Flora, he was raised on a farm in Missouri. His interest in drawing and art began during his earliest days at school. In High School, he drew and took photos for the school newspaper while taking night classes at the Academy of Fine Arts.

After volunteering for the Red Cross during the war, Walt started his career as an advertising cartoonist. But Kansas City wouldn't be enough to suit him for long. In 1923, he left for Hollywood with only his drawing materials and 40 dollars in his hands.

Walt joined his brother Roy in California, and they combined forces to start their production operation in their uncle's garage. Soon, they created the first 'Alice Comedy' short for a company in New York. Just a mere few years later, Walt would bring Mickey Mouse to life.

He is probably the most famous cartoon character in the world, but Mickey wasn't even Walt's OG. He created him as a replacement for Oswald the Lucky Rabbit after Universal took control of the character. But Walt, being Walt, didn't let this get him down. Instead, he began immediately working on our much-loved mouse friend, this time learning from his mistakes.

Mickey first appeared in Plane Crazy; however, since this didn't initially get picked up for distribution, his first public appearance was in the forever iconic Steamboat Willie. From there, Mickey quickly rose to fame, maintaining his popularity for the years to come.

There's a reason Walt's words, 'I hope we never lose sight of one thing, that it all started with a mouse,' gives us all goosebumps. Because after decades of many more adored animated characters, no one ever forgets when they fell in love with the mouse. It was very deserving when he became the first cartoon character to receive a star on the Hollywood Walk of Fame.

Walt then ventured out of film and sold the licensing for Mickey Mouse to be put on pencil tablets. Over the next 100 years, Mickey would go on to be seen just about anywhere. The most concentrated area is Lydia Steiner's bedroom. And I'm not even kidding about that. A couple of years ago, I had some unwanted mousey visitors in my flat, and they decided they wanted to hang out in my room.

Although this sounds like the set-up for one of my seriously effed-up sex dreams, the mice I found under my bed at 3 a.m. were very real. When the pest control man came to look, he opened my bedroom door and burst out laughing. He said it was no wonder they wanted to be in my room; it's like a mouse shrine.

He wasn't even exaggerating either; I had Mickey ears, prints, Disney World photos, and everything else Disney you can think of covering those walls. He couldn't believe I didn't want to keep the mice. I was like, 'Sir, if they're willing to wear a bow tie or sew me a ball gown, they can stay. If not, I'm going to start charging them lodge'. London rent prices are no joke.

Walt's love for innovating animation continued into the 30s when he introduced technicolour and the multiplane camera technique to his short films. With his first colour short, 'Silly Symphonies,' Walt earned the first of 22 personal Academy Awards, the record of the most Academy Awards in history.

He was commended for creating a working environment that made everyone feel involved. He didn't let his mistakes be failures. Instead, he learned from them and turned them into successes. He was truly committed to not only learning from other people but including them in the journey. He allowed anyone to contribute to his storyboards, knowing the best way to get the most extraordinary story was by collaboration.

When Pirates of the Caribbean was being built at Disneyland, Walt noticed a man from Louisiana working on the ride. He took the time to converse with the gentleman, asking him about his birthplace and if the ride truly represented it. They then went on a walk-through of the ride together, and when the man suggested that they add fireflies to one of the scenes, Walt instructed his Imagineers to install them immediately.

Since we're on the subject, Walt's first amusement park, Disneyland, opened in 1955—a huge milestone for the Disney company. There are now 12 Disney Parks worldwide, in America, France, and Asia. Walt Disney World, 'The Florida Project', was very close to Walt's heart and remains the largest resort after its opening in 1971. Sadly, Walt never got to see the opening of his passion project, as he passed away five years prior.

Before Walt lost his life, he became deeply invested in the establishment of the California Institute of the Arts, a college-level school of all creative learning and performing arts. He said, 'It's the principal thing I hope to leave when I move on to greener pastures. If I can help provide a place to develop the talent of the future, I think I will have accomplished something.' Walt did a lot to pave the way for future artists, and not just within the Disney company.

Walt's legacy certainly lives on, not only through his films and parks but also through the ever-expanding company, which has since seen new labels. This includes TV Networks, live-action TV and film, books, stage musicals, stores, home sites, cruise lines, streaming services, and so much more. If anything is a fact, it's that no matter how much the haters stamp their feet, Disney won't be going anywhere anytime soon.

Walt Disney has definitely earned his place as one of the most influential and committed figures in history. He is an easy man to admire. He came to California with a dream, but not even he could dream as big as this. Everyone loves a success story, and his is a pretty incredible one. We all need people to look up to in our lives. For me, Walt Disney is for sure one of them. He is quite literally the original Disney Adult.

Though Walt has had an undeniable lasting effect on the Disney company and animation, with it, he left some enormous shoes to fill. Two years after his death, his brother, Roy. O Disney was named CEO of the Walt Disney Company. Though they originally founded the company together, Walt was always in charge of the creative side.

Despite this, Roy chose to take on the responsibility that Walt had left behind. Since Walt Disney World was a project so close to Walt's heart, Roy postponed his retirement so he could see this through. Roy then lost his own life just two months after its opening.

Since he had been so heavily involved in Walt Disney World's initial operation, Roy's death devastated the new Cast Members. Morale around the park began to drop, and in a bid to bring everyone back together, an emergency meeting was held in Cinderella's Castle. This allowed employees to speak and give feedback. The company had to find a way to keep going without the Disney brothers.

Just as with Walt's passing, the company had to 'keep moving forward', as Walt had always strived to. Over the years, they would have a slate of many different CEOs. Donn Tatum, E.Cardon Walker, Ron Miller, Michael Eisner, Bob Iger, Bob Chapek, Bob Iger, Bob Iger, Bob Iger, Bob Iger, Bob Iger.

The stories behind these men are different in terms of their journey, experience and way into the company. Many worked for Disney for decades before ascending the throne, while others were directly related to the Disney family.

Despite the controversies that seem to follow the Disney CEOs, the company has not been denied great victories during these times. A lot has happened since the passing of the Disney Brothers, and among that is a lot of success.

Most of these CEOs were in power long before we graced the earth. I'd even bet you there are a lot of Disney Adults that couldn't tell you shit about who's in charge. Who gives a fuck about that corporate crap anyway? However, that all changed with Bob Iger - a name we all know and love. So why is it that suddenly everyone is so interested in Disney's CEO?

Having worked closely under Eisner, Iger became very ready to step into the spotlight. In his biography, 'The Ride of a Lifetime,' he talks in depth about his journey into this role, and it is definitely an inspiring path he has walked.

Bob Iger knew how to get things done, so he transformed Disney into one of the most admired and respected companies to work for. He was also the driving force behind the acquisition of Pixar, a massive milestone in Disney history. Iger even went as far as getting Oswald the Lucky Rabbit back. He led Disney to acquire Marvel and Lucasfilm and also opened Hong Kong Disneyland, Shanghai Disneyland, and Aulani.

Iger was championed as CEO, receiving numerous accolades to prove it. Yet, in the biggest plot twist of 2020 (the COVID lockdown can have a second place), he announced he was stepping down. Bob Chapek took over the reins and navigated a tough time for the company through the pandemic. Chapek had the difficult task of closing the theme parks, halting the cruise line and letting go of many employees.

This was just the start of bad times for Chapek, as he continued to anger the company and fans alike with his decisions.

None of them proved successful, and the numbers reflected this. As you can imagine, the suits were not happy.

Plot twist number two: Iger is back in the hot seat after barely having the time to miss the big man. Jesus Christ, he's giving me whiplash. Though he was initially contracted for just two years, he recently stated that he will definitely step down at the end of 2026.

Bob Iger was welcomed back with open arms by the company and fans alike. I, myself, was delighted to see his return. He knows what he is doing and is committed to Walt's craft and legacy. During his initial term as CEO, Iger promised to create memorable movies and characters, something which I hope he continues to commit to during his second term. We just want original content, ffs.

Disney Adults have been on a wild ride over the years with a slate of very different CEOs. And yet, it's still somewhat hard to tell when the cult of Disney Adults first began. Walt has had admirers ever since he started in the industry. But I'm not convinced people in the 1920s were queuing for hours for a popcorn bucket. Still, there were a large number of people tripping over themselves to get the Disney experience. The success of Snow White is the perfect example of this.

The company's long history means that different generations have been able to enjoy their work. People have been able to grow up loving Disney and then watch their children grow up loving Disney, and so, the Circle of Life goes on. I wonder if Walt relied on his fans being horny devils so they would birth him more fans. Whether he did or not, you can't fault the system.

This is a very loose summary of Walt and the Disney company. There is so much more to their history and story, which I will elaborate on in further chapters. But just from this snippet, you can see that Disney is so much more than a mouse or a castle. There is a lot of Disney to love, and it's unsurprising that it has such a dedicated fandom. That's you guys, by the way. Take a bloody bow.

The company's growth has only allowed it to appeal to a larger market, meaning there is more for everyone. This has made it easier for Disney Adults to drag people along for the ride. I can't tell you the number of times I have used Marvel or Star Wars as a selling point to draw people in, along with thrill rides or 'you can drink around the world!'. And before you know it, you're one Mickey Premium bar away from a lifelong addiction.

Despite the hate for Disney that exists, we know for a fact that Disney is here to stay. I'm going to bet they have another 100 years in them at an absolute minimum. So, people can scream at Disney Adults all they want, but we're here to stay—especially if Disney adults keep fornicating as they do.

Lydia's Sexiest Disney Characters Ranked:

1. Prince Eric.
2. Scar. If you've seen the stage musical you'll know what I mean.
3. Prince Naveen.
4. John Smith. Surprising, as I normally don't do blondes.
5. Shang.
6. Buzz Lightyear. You get it.
7. Flynn Rider.
8. Robin Hood. Don't you dare judge me.
9. Megara. She raised questions of confusion.
10. Gaston. This is my toxic trait.

Step 2: Love the Films

I feel like this is going to be **the** most obvious step. If you don't like Disney films, then you have no business being a Disney Adult. And no, that doesn't mean you have to like EVERY Disney film. It's precisely your opinion as a Disney Adult that makes you so damn interesting.

If my friend Jamie and I ever go missing at a house party, you can bet we're in the kitchen, with an open bottle of wine next to us - actually an empty bottle of wine - intensely debating recently released Disney films. I'm not even exaggerating when I say people have had to remove our drinks and us from each other during these heated discussions. If I hear that girl say one more time that there hasn't been a good Pixar film since Inside Out, I'm going to turn her inside out.

I promise I'm not a violent person. Not all the time. But it is this exact reaction that truly separates Disney Adults from Disney fans. I love nothing more than to spend my time dissecting Disney films and having heated discourse about the remakes and sequels. You should know I do have other hobbies too, like binge drinking. And debating Disney while binge drinking.

The best thing about Disney is that there are so many films to love. Even before you include the new franchises. When you look at fandoms that rival Disney, like Harry Potter or Studio Ghibli, they are but a fraction in comparison to Disney.

We're into our second century of Disney content now, and if the next century is half as good as the first, then it's going to be one hell of a ride. But before we get ahead of ourselves, just like when I talk about my boyfriend, let's talk about the Disney films that actually exist at the moment.

Walt Disney started animating long before his features. It all began with shorts and cartoons years before his first full-length movie: Snow White and the Seven Dwarves. Disney's first project to sell was 'Alice's Wonderland,' which wasn't dissimilar to the later story. It wasn't long before Walt and his brother Roy sold six more episodes entitled 'Alice Comedies.'

In order to make all this happen, they officially created the Disney company. Here, the Oswald the Lucky Rabbit series was born, and the following year, they would lose their contract. This, of course, was not the end of days; instead, it was something much different. As we know by now, this is what birthed the legend himself, Mickey friggin Mouse.

Walt spent the next decade animating Mickey Mouse stories, with his friends Minnie, Pluto, Donald, Daisy, and Goofy joining him along the way. Then came the ground-breaking release of Snow White.

The Disney Brothers have already made history with their work thus far, and we're only just getting to their first feature. Who was to predict what would go on to happen next? Although these old originals from Disney & Mickey Mouse are less popular in the contemporary world, since few people who experienced their release are still alive, there are those devout fans who still hold them close to their hearts. *cough* Disney Adults *cough*.

The next five years would be later deemed 'The Golden Era'. Walt had experienced overwhelming success from his films, and he wasn't going to let this momentum falter. And fuck me, am I glad he didn't! The next slate was Pinocchio, followed by Fantasia, Dumbo, and Bambi. The 5-minute long animated shorts that put Walt on the map were long forgotten. And we all know that anything longer than 5 minutes is always a good thing.

Subsequently, Disney entered a new era of storytelling. Mr. Disney was no longer looking for cheap laughs. Instead, he wanted a full-length narrative with a beginning, middle, and end—a story that made us all feel, even a story that would traumatise us. I've honestly gotten over breakups easier than the death of Bambi's mum.

Next came the 'Wartime Era', which unsurprisingly brought drastic changes for the studio. Just like many businesses, the Disney brothers took a hit. The loss of animators to military service and new release restrictions dramatically changed the style of movies that they were creating.

For example, The Three Caballeros was created as propaganda to strengthen the relationship between the USA and South America. This is a fact that anyone who has ever ridden the ride with me at EPCOT will already be aware of. As I've said before, I'm the one who will not be shy about explaining the history of a Disney ride. It's just unfortunate for everyone else that there's a margarita stand right near the ride, and therefore, my volume somewhat increases on this attraction. Lo siento.

As a result of this unusual period, other films from this era have become forgotten over time. Although we Disney Adults do what we can to keep their memory alive, it is unlikely that many other usual movie-goers would recognize many of the

thanks to the absolute legend that is Alan Menken. In 1995, they split the Original Score award into 2 categories: Dramatic and Comedy/ Musical. This wouldn't be the only time that The Academy made dramatic changes to its awards, which were suspected to prevent Disney from dominating. More on that in the next era.

As if we weren't spoilt enough in the 90s, it was Pixar's time to shine. Though Disney and Pixar had previously collaborated on computer-generated animation, it was agreed in 1991 that they would create and distribute a feature-length film. Four years later, Toy Story opened in cinemas and became the highest-grossing film of the year. Pixar could now say goodbye to the commercials they were previously making, and instead focus on creating feature films. Toy Story 2 and Bugs Life were released later in the 90s, once again to commercial success.

The noughties brought a new century and with it, the hope of new ideas. This was the real modern world; anyone could be who they wanted to be. Well, they could, but they'd be abused about it online. *cough* Disney Adults *cough*. It was time to say goodbye to the 20th century and, alongside it, no more war, discrimination or... haha, sorry, if only that were true. But no matter how big the dreams seemed for the new century, Disney was dreaming even bigger.

The millennium age was the new world, and now was the time to take risks. Hence, 'The Experimental Era.' This was the new age of animation. 3D animation had already made its debut in the mid-90s with Toy Story, and Pixar was paving the way for the unique style. Something Disney wanted to take inspiration from. However, Pixar was now a strong box office contender, and with the launch of DreamWorks, this was no longer a one-horse race.

Fantasia, Dinosaur, The Emperor's New Groove, Atlantic: Lost Empire, Lilo & Stitch, Treasure Planet, Brother Bear, Home on the Range, Chicken Little, Meet the Robinsons, and Bolt were all released in the next nine years, showing that Disney was not only refusing to slow down but instead speeding up. We moved from fairytales and fantasy to science fiction and other worlds. Times were changing, and fast.

Yet despite their determination, that decade, Pixar released some of the most immensely popular films in history: Monsters Inc, Finding Nemo, The Incredibles, Cars, Ratatouille, Wall. E, and Up. If that wasn't going to make Disney go SHIT, I don't know what was. And as much as I love him, I'm not even going to bring up that green ogre.

However, this guided us nicely into 'The Revival Era.' After The Princess and the Frog, Disney fully embraced CGI animation and started to try a new approach to their films and narrative. After the success of Pixar's movies, their robust scripts, and then Toy Story becoming the first animated film to receive a Best Original Screenplay nomination, Disney was influenced to try the same. They took a whole new approach to the films that were already in development. Instead of using the traditional model, like calling their films Rapunzel or The Snow Queen, they decided to rename them the more original and alluring: Tangled and Frozen.

This was only part of what Disney was doing to reclaim their place in the animated race (warzone). They began developing more in-depth characters, including plot twists and rewriting the predictable storyline of damsels and romance. Instead, they created heroes out of both genders and protagonists with more intrinsic goals.

Disney not only managed to pull this off, but they did it with astounding success. I don't need to tell you how much of a hit Frozen was. We all have the song burnt in our memory for the rest of time. Disney continued with this line of action with the rest of the films in this era: Winnie-the-Pooh, Wreck-It Ralph, Big Hero 6, Moana, Zootopia, and sequels, including Frozen 2 and Ralph Breaks the Internet.

Animated films were taking cinemas by storm. It went from Disney releasing their movies every couple of years, to multiple animated films from different studios premiering in the same year. It became its own genre and a competitive one at that. Until this point, The Academy was resistant to creating an award solely for animation. They had always argued that there weren't enough contenders. Yet, as we reached the 2000s, this was no longer the case.

Many feel the creation of the Best Animated Feature award was to prevent these films from taking the Best Picture spot, which Beauty & the Beast came very close to in the early 90s. Whether this is the case or not, it has provided animated films with a platform for recognition. Prior to this accolade, the Disney company had only been presented with special recognition awards for their achievement in animation instead of an official category.

As we all know, animation is no longer the frontrunner of the Disney film studios. They have never created more live-action, and I'm not just talking about the remakes. The noughties saw these films reach the peak of their success with The Pirates of the Caribbean and Narnia franchises. Oh, and let's not forget yet another Herbie movie. I couldn't possibly forget that one.

What's more, Disney Channel's original movies stepped into the spotlight—or, I should say, they convinced me to. There are videos of me singing High School Musical that will haunt me for the rest of my life. The commercial success of the High School Musical films, as well as Hannah Montana: The Movie, highlighted Disney's capabilities in all areas of filmmaking.

Though many would disagree, we still technically remain in the revival era. Nothing official has been established to argue this, but it's also believed we have to be in a new time. Fans have established terms such as 'the remake era', 'the post-revival era', and 'the Disney+ era'. None of which would be incorrect. It cannot be ignored that the Disney company has undergone a lot of changes since the millennium.

Disney has since purchased Pixar and, therefore, obtained more creative control over the company. There is also now a distribution deal with DreamWorks, and all of its films are released through Touchstone going forward. Disney has acquired many franchises, including Marvel, Avatar, and Lucasfilm (creator of the Star Wars and Indiana Jones franchises). This is a massive step in Disney becoming a larger film studio instead of exclusively an animation studio. They now have power over some of the largest film franchises in the world.

In 2010, we saw the start of one of Disney's most controversial moves yet. The live-action remakes. Of course, when this began, it wasn't contentious at all; instead, it was an exciting step for Disney and its filmmaking. Alice in Wonderland was the first film to receive a modern adaptation. I say modern because, in 1996, 101 Dalmatians was the first ever Disney animated movie to get a live-action remake. Glenn Close's Cruella De Vil received a high reception, even reprising the role in a sequel.

Alice in Wonderland was also a very successful remake, with its own sequel many years later. However, Disney took a different approach. This time, they had Alice return to Wonderland as a teenager. The same would apply to Disney's following live-action films, The Sorcerer's Apprentice and Maleficent. Both have striking differences from their original animated versions and instead present a fresh and original perspective.

These would go on to spark a new trend that Disney would cling to over the next 10+ years. Cinderella, released in 2015, was the first remake to almost identically duplicate the original story, and it still received positive reviews. Many of the live-action films that would be released over the years would have the same reaction.

Fans, myself included, enjoyed seeing their favourite stories come to life—quite literally, many years after they relished them the first time. It also allowed some of our favourite and most well-known stars to take on iconic characters. I've really enjoyed getting to experience new songs added to the soundtrack, most commonly by the original composer. My boy Menken still got it.

However, Disney continued to use the same formula for the films it produced in the years that followed. In fact, Disney has now released a whopping 23 live-action remakes, with many more already being filmed, announced, and in development.

Now, I may seem negative as I break down this new Era of Disney, and I honestly don't mean to be. On the whole, I love the Disney remakes despite them not quite hitting the spot like the others. Not that this is always the case. The recent release of The Little Mermaid in 2023 was, in my opinion, one of the best to come from Disney.

I don't have a problem with remakes—I embrace them. My problem lies with the amount being rushed out and the lack of original content. Over the years, there have been some excellent Walt Disney Studios releases, like Encanto. But when you look at

Disney's releases in the last ten years, it's tough to distinguish the original content between Marvel, Star Wars, and Pixar.

In spite of all of this, Disney's new age has brought some exciting things along with it. What has been built with Walt Disney's legacy will go down in history, not to mention the impact it has had on the film industry and storytelling as an art form. As we enter the streaming world with Disney+ and other providers, the way we consume this content has changed forever.

I genuinely love being able to watch any Disney film at a press of a button - no, really - I fucking love it, but I also love going to the cinema and immersing myself in its world. I swear there is no better way to experience the animation than on the big screen. The songs will never sound as good as they do out of those sound systems, and I absolutely love being able to lob popcorn at kids when they talk during the wrong bits. That's probably my favourite part.

Exciting films are coming up that have superheroes, are animated, and are set a long time ago in a galaxy far, far away. All of which I cannot wait for. And as for that original content? Don't worry. Disney will come to their senses and one day hire me to write them a bomb-ass fairytale film. I won't even include profanity in it. Not fucking much, anyway.

Lydia's Saddest Disney Scenes

1. Mufasa's death. I'm actually crying even writing it down.
2. 'Take her to the moon for me.' Bing Bong. Chills. Literal Chills.
3. Todd the fox left in the woods in Fox & the Hound. Honestly, I think a lot of my teenage therapy was as a result of this.
4. The first 10 minutes of Up. I don't need to say anymore.
5. Baby Mine scene in Dumbo.
6. Sully says goodbye to Boo.
7. Baymax's sacrifice. It was sadder than when the brother died, and you know it.
8. 'When she loved me'. You don't need me to tell you the film.
9. Toy Story 3. I know I said scenes, but I make the fucking rules.
10. Stitch and The Ugly Duckling book.

Step 3: Obsess over the Parks

"Disneyland is dedicated to the ideals, the dreams, and the hard facts that have created America—with the hope that it will be a source of joy and inspiration to all the world." This is a segment from Walt's opening-day speech at the first Disney Park in California. I can only imagine that, at the time, this declaration felt somewhat ambitious. Little did the public know this was precisely what would come to be.

When 1955 brought the opening of Disneyland, the Disney company was well into its success with its feature-length movies. So, where did the connection between films and amusement parks come from? Don't worry. You know damn well I'm going to tell you.

Walt spent a lot of time at the fairground with his daughters, spending quality time with them when he wasn't busy creating the best bloody films ever. Because Walt is, well, Walt, it wasn't ever going to stop there. He looked around at what most people would perceive now to be a cheap, trashier day out and thought about how he could turn it into somewhere adored by both children and adults. Yep, you read that right, fucking adults.

Walt wanted to create a place he could enjoy with his own family, amongst others, that was more than just lights and a carousel. Here, the world's first-ever 'theme park' was born.

The discrepancy between the terms theme park and amusement park has become much looser over the years. Yet, Disney Parks are still set at a completely different level, and this chapter will break down exactly why.

The opening of Disneyland was a hot mess. I'm talking Will Smith slapping Chris Rock at the Oscars kind of a hot mess. There were forged tickets, too many guests, and not enough stock. Everything fell apart. It was like an Ann Summer's sale the day before Valentine's Day.

With Disneyland being the first of its kind, it was always going to feel experimental. Walt spent a lot of time evaluating his mistakes and making sure they weren't replicated. This attitude would be maintained for all of his Disney Parks.

Much of the original Disney Park remains from the opening day; you can even ride some of the same attractions. But it's impossible to oversee how the park has evolved. Through the years, Disney has wholly transformed both its own theme parks and the theme park culture all over the world.

Nevertheless, none of this should be taken for granted. This was a challenging process for Walt. When he first proposed the concept of a theme park, he had next to no support. Banks refused to lend money, and even his brother Roy wasn't convinced it would be a good idea. Despite all of this, Walt persevered, believing the potential was there. After a good fight, he eventually managed to get financial support from ABC in exchange for Walt presenting a regular TV show. It would be here he would share his magical ideas with the world.

Walt fell in love with Disneyland, spending as much time there as he could. He even hosted leaders from all around the world. But we know Walt, and he was already planning his next move. Just a few years later, Walt would begin developing his next dream, the secret 'Florida Project'. Have you got goosebumps? I have goosebumps.

He purchased large sections of land in Orlando, selected for its climate. He had a big dream, and he needed a big place to do it. This new park was not only going to right everything that he had gotten wrong with Disneyland but so much more. Disney World was the plan, but his ideas of innovation far exceeded that.

Devastatingly, Walt never saw the opening of the next park. He lost his life just a year after announcing 'The Florida Project' to the press. But this time, his brother Roy was going to back him until the end. Magic Kingdom (a much larger version of the Disneyland park), along with three resorts and golf courses, opened in 1971. Roy dedicated this park to his brother, his final wish coming to life. In his honour, the name was changed from Disney World to Walt Disney World.

This time around, they knew exactly what they were doing. They opened in the lower season of October to prevent an overhaul of guests. The actual grand opening ceremony was saved until the end of October, giving them time to fix any teething problems. Crowds started small in the beginning, within ten thousand. By the end of the opening ceremonies, Magic Kingdom had seen over 400,000 guests.

Roy knew that this park was always going to be more than just one kingdom. The location had been meticulously planned for accessibility, placing it between two major Orlando highways. The surrounding area was ready for more infrastructure and expansions.

Roy was insistent that Walt's vision became a reality. Shortly after Walt's death, he told the WED staff (the team in charge of developing the parks, more on this to come) that "we're going to finish the Florida park, and we're going to do it just the way Walt wanted it." Roy did everything to ensure Walt's dreams were secured just before he lost his own life the year of the Walt Disney World opening.

The loss of the Disney Brothers was heartbreaking, but their legacy couldn't have been in better hands. In 1982, the EPCOT Center opened, dedicated to international culture and technological innovation. This was another passion project of Walt Disney himself, and although he envisioned a literal utopian urban city to function here, the park is instead dedicated to those ideals. And though I'd sell many of my organs on the black market for a chance to live in the city that Walt dreamed up, getting shitfaced on World Showcase will have to do for now.

EPCOT is an acronym for Every Pint Comes Out Terrific. You guys know that is fucking true. Yet, as accurate as it is, EPCOT actually stands for Experimental Prototype Community of Tomorrow. Initially, it was comprised of two sections: Futureworld and World Showcase. However, it recently went through an extensive overhaul that split it into four parts: World Discover, World Celebration, World Nature, and World Showcase. Recognised by its geodesic sphere, the home to the ride Spaceship Earth, EPCOT is the first of the Disney locations to be identified by something other than a castle. And yet you know it, and I know it, it's a giant golf ball.

The park has become very popular for both Space lovers and booze lovers. And although I love a good planet, my favourite part of EPCOT is definitely immersing myself in the cultures (cocktails) of World Showcase. But here, Disney once again shows that they can create a space (pun intended) that all different people with passions for all different things love.

This time, Disney wasn't going to wait as long to expand the dream. However, in an unexpected twist of events, they were now taking it overseas and out of the USA for the first time. Tokyo Disneyland opened in 1983 and is styled similarly to Magic Kingdom & Disneyland. The Oriental Land Company licensed the theme from The Walt Disney Company, making them the owners of the park. With a few minor changes, this park still incorporates everything that makes a Disney Park a Disney Park.

Disney had now branched out internationally and was bringing its parks to other cultures. However, it wasn't going to neglect the OGs back in America. Hollywood Studios (formerly known as Disney-MGM Studios) was being constructed to open in 1989 in Florida. This park pays homage to classic Hollywood in the 1930s and 40s, when the Disney brothers were starting in the industry.

Hollywood Studios has seen a mass of changes over the years, its centrepiece being one of them. It originally started out being known by the Earrfel Tower, a faux water tower. This was then replaced by the Sorcerer's Hat, just like the one Mickey wears in Fantasia, which I was despondent to say goodbye to. The Chinese Theatre, just like that in actual Hollywood, is now the main visual piece of Hollywood Studios. However, many fans more commonly recognise the Tower of Terror to be the park icon.

The studios are, of course, dedicated to Hollywood. However, Michael Eisner, Disney's CEO at the time, said that this was more about the state of mind rather than the place on a physical map. This has carried through to the modern day, as the park continues to celebrate some of Disney's - and the world's - most popular films and franchises.

The park started as a working film studio and backlot, which guests could visit to experience actual film-making. Over the years, the stages have been transformed into rides and other film-related attractions.

As film-making continues to develop and change through time, so does Hollywood Studio's commemoration of these stories. Both classic film and modern franchises are celebrated alike in the park. That old-style Hollywood is still very much felt throughout, and yet with that, there is also some of the most advanced ride technology. I mean, by this point, you guys know I'm a raging nerd, but fuck me, this park really brings it out of me.

The same year, Disney filed a trademark for the term 'Imagineering'. Why is this important, you may ask? Well, the Imagineers are the reason we have Disney Parks at all. This brings us back to WED, which was initially named after Walt Elias Disney but is now known as Imagineers. WED was formed before the opening of Disneyland to bring to life the vision of Walt's parks.

This company is the brain behind it all and has conducted all the research into their development. The company is composed of the 'Imagineers', the term coming from Imagination Engineering. They are everything from the architects, designers, show writers, and graphic designers behind the artistic creation of the Disney Parks and their attractions.

WED Enterprises was officially renamed Walt Disney Imagineering in 1986 and has become a term that all Disney fans have become familiar with. It is this group of people that shows the level of detail that Disney is willing to go to and how committed they are to their guest's experience. Walt was very encouraging of innovation within the parks, even himself commenting on how Disneyland will never be finished as long as there is imagination. I'm super happy that this has remained true with the ever-expanding and modernisation of the Disney Parks.

Ex-Disney Imagineers have shared that there are 15 principles of Disney Imagineering in the Imagineering pyramid. These fall into five different tiers. It includes things like attention to detail, hidden Mickeys, forced perspective, and it all begins with a story. This is precisely what makes an attraction a DISNEY attraction.

All these sections lead us up to tier 1, which is Walt's cardinal rule. This consists of a single fundamental practice that Imagineers refer to as 'plussing'. Now, we've already delved a lot into Walt and who he was. Therefore, it should come as no surprise now that Plussing is constantly asking yourself, "How do I make this better?" Walt never stopped challenging himself to be able to give us more. And for that, I love him dearly.

Places throughout Europe have inspired some of Disney's most well-known stories. Therefore, it didn't surprise anyone, like at all, that the next Disney Park would find its way there. Originally opening as Euro Disney but later renamed the more geographically accurate Disneyland Paris, the park opened its gates to the public in 1992.

This shouldn't come as a shock to many, as it feels like Disneyland Paris has been celebrating an anniversary of some sort every year since it opened. Which I don't disrespect; if I could decorate a castle for my birthday every year, I sure as shit would. This park was also built on the original Disneyland design. However, this time, it boasted Sleeping Beauty's castle instead of Cinderella's.

Next, Walt Disney World would receive its fourth and final

theme park, Animal Kingdom. The largest theme park in the world. This theme was predictable because it was also inspired by more of Walt's ideas. Initially, the classic ride Jungle Cruise was meant to consist of **real** animals. The reality of this at the time was that it was impossible to do safely, and instead, WED's animatronics were used in the attraction. But this would not be the end of Walt's animal dreams, because here comes Joe Rohde.

Joe has become a fan favourite among Disney Adults. This is not only because of his brilliance but also because of the way he thinks outside the box. The perfect example of this was his idea to bring a real-life 400-pound Bengel tiger to his Animal Kingdom meeting with Michael Eisner—a move that has Walt Disney written all over it.

Once again, the Imagineers went above and beyond for this park. They travelled to Asia and Africa to study the landscapes and wildlife. They even collected seeds from 37 countries to be used for the vegetation in the park. Disney committed itself to the care and conservation of the species they adopted for the park, hiring staff from 69 zoos around the USA to look after their new animals.

Joe Rohde and his Imagineers took their new responsibility very seriously. They sought advice from many professionals and attended numerous meetings of the Association of Zoos & Aquariums. Disney's Animal Kingdom was shaping up to be more than just a theme park. Instead, it was a place to educate people about our role in taking action for our planet. This led to the creation of the Disney Conservation Fund, which has since become a leader in international conservation.

Animal Kingdom would complete the theme parks at Walt Disney World after the addition of 2 water parks. Blizzard Beach takes the form of a melted ski resort. Hence, there are water slides and a working ski lift. Typhoon Lagoon then replaced its predecessor, River Country, and is based on a tropical shipwreck. Both are themed brilliantly and are a great addition to a Walt Disney World holiday. Also, Blizzard Beach plays Christmas songs all year round, of which I am entirely supportive. Fuck the Scrooges.

Despite the completion of Walt Disney World's new parks, Disney Park's history was still ongoing. It was time to go back to the original park for its expansion. Disney's California Adventure opened up next to Disneyland in Anaheim. Though initially announced to be WestCOT, another version of EPCOT, the company dramatically changed its mind. Instead came a park dedicated to California, with a man-made mountain in the shape of its native animal: the Grizzly Bear.

2001 was a big year for second theme parks, as Tokyo Disneyland received its second Disney park, Tokyo DisneySea. Not only was this the most expensive theme park ever built, but it has also become a fan favourite. DisneySea is regularly referred to as both Disney's best theme park and the best theme park in the world. Disney is the gift that just keeps giving.

Continuing in 2002, as Disney was not going to leave anyone out, Disneyland Paris got their second park. Like before, this was planned to be a copy of another Disney park - MGM Studios. Though still considered a sister park to Hollywood Studios, with the same concepts, the Walt Disney Studios Park has taken its own shape, incorporating original ideas and unique experiences. At every Disney Park in the world, there is something unique there that cannot be experienced at another park. This one was going to be no exception.

However, the rest of Asia wasn't going to be neglected either, and they were about to wave their arms in the air and want a bit of that Disney-loving. Which they were definitely going to get. Hong Kong Disneyland opened in 2005, the first Asian Disney park outside of Tokyo. Although this was the fifth Disneyland-style theme park, with similar attractions and the castle feature, it was again going to also brag about its unique attractions.

Disney Parks would go quiet for a while now. Though constantly working on their existing parks, with new attractions, developments, and expansions, there would be no new park for 11 years. That was until 2016 came along, bringing with it the twelfth and final Disney Park. Shanghai Disneyland Park promised 'authentically Disney and distinctly Chinese'. There were lots of changes made to the original Disneyland formula, and Chinese architects and designers were brought in to bring their culture to the Disney design.

It has now been eight years since the opening of a new Disney Park, and there are no publicly known plans for this to change. Will there be more Disney Parks in the future? It's very possible. Disney has waited longer than this in the past to bring more magic to the world. But this doesn't mean that the Imagineers have packed up their stuff and gone home. They never stop working on improving the guest experience at the parks, with many new changes coming in the near future, including whole new areas themed on Frozen and Zootopia (to name just a couple).

One of the things I admire most about the Disney Parks is that no matter how often you visit, there is always something new to experience. Whether it's a new festival at EPCOT, a new meet-and-greet, a new ride, or a new seasonal activity, it's constantly evolving and always new.

So, though I love the original attractions and will always

love going back and experiencing them again, there is always something new waiting for me. The haters are going to say, why do you want to keep going back to the same place over and over again? Well, not only because it's utterly amazing, but there is always something different to encounter.

Throughout the seasons, the Disney Parks transform entirely. Halloween becomes Christmas overnight, and Disney celebrates every event and tradition. As I already said, there's always some kind of anniversary to celebrate at Disneyland Paris. And it's never just limited to one day. Walt Disney World's 50th anniversary was celebrated over 18 months. It did get extended due to the COVID-19 pandemic messing up their plans, but who wouldn't want to celebrate for even longer? You've heard it here first: if I make it to 50 (if an indecent number of Mickey premium bars haven't killed me first), it's going to be a celebration for at least 18 months.

Imagineers go into great detail with the parks and are very dedicated to them. Walt himself spent a lot of time in Disneyland observing the guests so he could iron out the minor kinks.

He didn't like that characters from other themed areas had to walk through lands that didn't match their characters. He felt it ruined the park's authenticity, and he wanted the experience to feel as immersive as possible.

This was no problem for Walt; he would surely have a simple solution. He suggested that Walt Disney World be built on top of a network of tunnels that Cast Members could use to navigate the park. So next time you're walking through Main Street USA, think about the fact that you're actually 2-3 levels up.

Walt wasn't going to stop there. He went as far as to sit and watch guests litter in the park. This wasn't for him to scald them or tell them off, which would have been my approach. Instead, he wanted to work out how long people would hold onto their rubbish before they gave up and dropped it. He worked out that, on average, people would drop their trash after 30 steps. It was then decided that there was to be a trash can at most 30 feet away from the previous one in every single park. This dramatically reduced the amount of litter in the park, keeping it cleaner, more sustainable, and easier for the custodial staff to maintain.

The park's team ensured that the trash cans always fit in with the theming of the area they're placed in and blend in with the backgrounds so they don't stand out. This has led to Disney trash cans having their own fandom; yes, that is the truth. I told you Disney Adults are wild. People not only admire their theming but also get a kick out of using them to eat off in Disney parks. I never said we were smart.

Gum cannot be bought at any Disney Park because Walt wanted to prevent it from getting stuck to the ground. We all know how gum gets everywhere and is nearly impossible to remove, and he wanted to maintain the aesthetic of the Disney Parks.

Walt Disney World became the first theme park in the world to play ambient music to create an immersive feeling. They pump smells around the park to allure guests. 20,000 different paints were used in WDW. Forced perspectives are used to make Cinderella Castle look taller and Main Street USA longer. Honestly, guys, I could go on and on here.

Your Disney experience also isn't limited to the theme parks. Not only do you have the Disney Aulani Resort in Hawaii, a perfect relaxing escape away from the theme park madness, but there's also the cruise line. There are currently five ships operating: Disney Magic, Disney Wonder, Disney Dream, Disney

Fantasy, and Disney Wish. Disney Treasure, Disney Adventure and Disney Destiny are the newbies that will be joining in the next couple of years. There will be another new, currently unnamed, ship that will join the fleet in 2028.

These cruises visit many destinations worldwide, including Africa, Alaska, Asia, the Bahamas, the Caribbean, Europe, Canada, Oceania, and Latin America. Disney even owns a private island, Castaway Cay, in the Bahamas, which is exclusive to Disney ships. Lookout Cay at Lighthouse Point, a new destination in the Bahamas, opened in the summer of this year.

These ships are a great way to immerse yourself in the Disney Magic, with characters and unique dining and attractions on board. You get to experience shows you can't anywhere else and food you can't get in any of the parks. All of this before you've even stepped off the ship.

Hey, if that isn't enough for you, there's always Adventures by Disney. You can take small ship trips, land adventures, and city escapes. I wouldn't tell anyone if I won the lottery, but there would be signs. And by signs, I mean I would immediately book the Disney Parks Around the World – Private Jet Adventure. Yes, that is precisely what you think it is.

For a cheeky $144,955+, you can take a jet to all the Disney Parks in the world in just 25 days. There are even added extras like the Taj Mahal and the Pyramids of Giza. This might be the ultimate dream for all Disney Adults. And though I would have to work 24 hours a day for the rest of my life just to pay the deposit, a girl can dream.

Disney Vacation Club may be a more financially viable route for those who want regular luxury holidays at Disney. Which, of course, I fucking do. But since the starting price to get yourself into the club is more than a deposit on a Zone 3 flat in London,

I still don't think I'm going to quite make the cut.

However, for those who are interested, DVC is Disney's timeshare programme that allows customers to invest in their properties and buy points that can be exchanged for Disney holidays all over the world, including the Adventures by Disney trips. It is possible to buy points from DVC members, which may make those Deluxe resorts feel that tiny bit more feasible. But for now, I'm just minimising my dating pool to DVC members only. This isn't really a problem, as there's no fucker in my dating pool anyway.

Revisiting the Disney Parks over the years has become one of my favourite things to do, which is a brave statement considering how offended people get by this. I constantly get asked things like, don't you get bored? Don't you get fed up going to the same place? I don't actually Debra, I've been to 9 nations in 1 day, when I know for a fact you've been to Benidorm 6,473 times since you were old enough to say Sticky Vicky.

So whether it's Asia, America, Paris, or the resort in Hawaii, I hope you all get to be told to have a magical day at one of the parks real soon. At the same time, it's also completely fine to sit in your bedroom, put the resort TV on YouTube, grab your Mickey ears, and spark a dream that we're meant to follow...

Lydia's Favourite WDW Disney Rides

1. Flight of Passage.
2. Rise of the Resistance. I know it's super clichè of me to go for the new ones, but I can't even pretend like they're not awesome.
3. Seven Dwarfs Mine Train. Don't you fucking judge me.
4. Thunder Mountain.
5. Kilimanjaro Safari's.
6. Soarin'. I have a foot fetish.
7. Pirates of the Caribbean. For the sniff.
8. Slinky Dog Dash. I'm a wuss when it comes to rollercoasters.
9. The Haunted Mansion. I honestly love the queue as much as the ride.
10. It's a Small Word. Controversial, I know. But I'm honestly so sadistic that I get off on everyone hating this ride.

Step 4: Have All the Merch

It's been over 12 years since Primark launched its first Disney range. The second they got that licensing, the much-loved shop went seriously hard with its clothes & home line. Which, as you can probably predict, the haters really hated.

Immediately, they ran to social media to moan about how all their apparel now had pictures of Mickey Mouse and Stitch all over them. They're asking the world, who the hell is causing **trouble** and actually buying all this Disney crap from Primark? And I sit there with an evil smile.

Honestly, Primark going all out on Disney was one of the best things that happened to the shop. Now, I can fill my wardrobe with Disney attire at an affordable price because we all know that sometimes the Disney Store can break the bank. I look at the price tags and think, 'Why would someone pay $50 for a Starbucks cup?' she says with her Mickey Ears, Spirit Jersey, and Mickey Converse on. Me, that's also me.

Owning something Disney is not unusual. In fact, Disney has grown so large that it has found a way to be ever-present in our lives. A lot of that is due to the merchandise that has flooded the world. I challenge you to go to any shopping centre, food court, or very public place and not see someone wearing or displaying something Disney.

Walt, being the genius businessman he was, saw the opportunity to merchandise Mickey Mouse pretty soon after his creation. It wasn't long before the beloved characters began not only popping up as teddies and toys, but all sorts of other items. It was here that Walt realised that by licensing the copyright to the characters, he could bring in more money that he could reinvest into his film-making.

Over the years, the wildly popular Disney films have spawned many products that people of all ages have taken home to love. Winnie-the-Pooh became one of the most popular nursery designs for newborns, and children couldn't wait to wear the outfits of their favourite characters.

This was only going to escalate as the films became more popular. You only have to look to the ice legend herself, Elsa.

Frozen smashed the box office, and you'd be hard-pressed to find many children who didn't have Frozen on their Christmas wish list in the year of its release. The situation escalated so severely that many of the products were completely sold out, leaving children devastated that they were not able to wear Elsa's wig or Anna's dress on Christmas morning. But I promise you no one was more pissed off about the situation than me. Did I want scented candles in my stocking that Christmas morning? Fuck no. I wanted to glide around in an Elsa wig.

Now, I know what you're thinking. You're talking an awful lot about children here. Well, initially, the aim of merchandising these films was to sell toys, and the target market was, of course, children.

Now, calm down. Don't start carving your Mickey Ears into weapons just yet because even Disney saw an opportunity here. Although the target audience was little ones, they were also aimed toward the adult market since it was going to be their money paying for it. However, there was undeniably a market for adults to begin buying products for themselves. Remember what Walt said, "I do not make films primarily for children. I make them for the child in all of us, whether we be six or sixty."

All of a sudden, Disney clothes appeared in adult sizes, board games and Lego sets were intended for older consumers, and Disney kitchen sets grew in popularity. You're telling me that a young Disney lover doesn't have a Minnie Mouse tea towel set on their wish list? It's now reached the point that you could quite possibly buy any household item that is Disney-themed. And I know that because I have.

First of all, let's talk about official Disney merchandise. This is anything sold by Disney itself, either in a Disney Store, in one of the parks, or by the newly restored online Disney Store. Initially, Disney products could only be bought in the Disney Stores, and the park merchandise was sold separately at the parks. However, now they are used interchangeably, and many of the items can be found online.

This doesn't mean that all the products will be accessible everywhere; there are still unique things you can buy at Disney Parks that you can't buy anywhere else. However, it has made it easier for Disney Adults to get the items their hearts desire.

Over the years, the items sold in the Disney Parks have become collectors' items. What initially started as souvenirs that you would commonly find in holiday gift shops, like mugs, keyrings, and pressed pennies, has now developed into so much more.

The original merchandise from decades ago is now kept safely in The Walt Disney Archives, although some remain in circulation and are very much collector's items for Disney Adults. You can also find some on display at One Man's Dream in Hollywood Studios.

It would be easy to detect these collector's items due to their ageing and more dated design. However, a keen eye would notice that they would instead have the name 'Walt Disney Productions' on them, as that was the corporate name used on merchandise until 1986. Therefore, you know anything that displays that name is going to be worth stealing. I mean buying.

Disney collectable items aren't just limited to archived souvenirs from the parks. Disneyana is an umbrella term for a wide variety of Disney collectables, from toys to animation cels (transparent sheets with hand-drawn animation). Disneyana is not a trademarked term by Disney; instead, it is technically the oldest existing Disney fan club. There is a website dedicated to selling these collectable items, and they are listed in their own category on eBay.

As time has passed, specific souvenirs have become more iconic. The obvious one which cannot possibly go unrecognised is Mickey Ears. And trust me, you're going to love the history of how they came to be.

After The Mickey Mouse Club aired on television with all the cast wearing Mickey Ears, everyone wanted to have them. These were the original designs of circular caps to which the ears are attached, as opposed to a headband. They were created by Roy Williams, an artist and entertainer on the television show.

These were immediately rolled out on the market to everyone who was clawing to get their hands on them. Now, the most interesting part about this is that the ears were initially designed for adults. HA, yes, adults. A different design, with a smaller cap, then had to be created for children. The famous Mickey Ears were initially designed for adults. ADULTS. Man, I love that.

In the 1980s, the caps turned into headbands and were, without a doubt, a huge success for the company. Since then, they have been one of the best-selling souvenirs at the parks, and those who visit Disney will rarely return without them. The designs have developed over the years and are ever-changing, with different themes and characters. They have become beloved by Disney Adults and will continue to be for generations to come.

Mugs, t-shirts, photo albums, and postcards are all still extremely popular in the parks, with seasonal lines and speciality items for celebrations and different events. It can become very addictive to want to stay on top of the merch and all the new stuff that comes out. More recently, Spirit Jerseys have risen in popularity due to their unique Disney Parks design. Lounge Fly bags are also adored by Disney Adults, and many people are known to collect them by the hundreds.

As beautiful as these items are, I have to put all my efforts into not buying everything. My credit limit will not allow it. Especially not the $37,500 jewelled Cinderella Castle ornament you can buy on Main Street USA. There isn't enough time in the world for me to take the feet pics that would be needed for me to afford that. Unfortunately, money doesn't grow on trees, not even Disney magic can convince us of that, but there are cheaper alternatives.

Other items have become popular over the years, including more affordable things like pressing pennies, pin trading, and collecting character autographs. Souvenirs don't always have to be pricey. We've even taken t-shirts to be signed by characters before to prevent having to buy ones from the Disney shops.

Now that Disney licenses its characters and designs, Disney products are popping up all over the place, and not just in

Primark. Many supermarkets all over the world sell Disney merchandise and souvenirs. Whenever I'm in Orlando, I always check Walmart and Target first for the merch I want. There are also character outlets that sell defunct merchandise from the parks at super affordable prices. Content creators online will regularly update you on the stock so you can be ready to grab whatever it is that you're after.

You could also buy things second-hand. Many people will sell their pre-loved items for a fair price, which is typically an excellent way for people to be able to collect things. There have been many times I have bought stuff I love from people that I would never be able to buy new.

Being friends with Disney Adults does have its perks. Take my cousin, for example, whose boyfriend refused to move in with her if she didn't offload some of her Disney mugs. This was the perfect situation as I got a shit ton of free Disney mugs, and Beth has plenty of space to fill with new mugs next time we go to Disney. Everyone wins. Except for Beth's boyfriend, but he doesn't need to know that.

Disney has now become so popular that people have literally built businesses around it. There are a wealth of small businesses that make Disney products and sell items for trips. Etsy is a great place to start to support these businesses. You will also find them advertised on Instagram and Facebook, and it's always best to purchase directly from the business so you know they aren't losing lots of money to listing fees. Support small businesses guys!

There are so many out there, and if I could list them all, I really would, but some of the ones I love at the moment are Becoming a Nerd, Ohana Kingdom, Autumn Always, Happy Place Print, Gleam and Glimmer Co., Happily Ever Threads,

Rope Drop Design, The Lost Bros, and Park Aesthetic Co.

It's not just the Walt Disney Studios films that Disney have merchandised the shit out of. Marvel and Star Wars have generated billions of revenue with the products that have come from their movies. There isn't a Star Wars fan out there who doesn't love to whack their lightsaber out at any given opportunity. Well, it's not just Star Wars fans, but that's a whole different conversation.

Some of the most iconic merchandise doesn't even come from Disney itself. Think Lego, think Funko Pops. Both are collector's items, and both are hugely popular with film fans who like to collect them, no matter their age.

Over the years, popcorn buckets have garnered a fan base. You can buy these buckets in the parks and refill them as many times as you like for a small additional fee. Who doesn't love a souvenir and a snack?

These buckets have become extremely popular for their theming, along with the fact that every park has an original design you can collect. Guests have been tripping over themselves to get the newest designs, to the point where people have queued for hours to try and get the latest releases. Who's ever going to forget when EPCOT released their Figment popcorn bucket back in 2022?

Figment is one of the mascots for EPCOT, known for the Journey into Imagination ride. Although this ride has had a wobbly past of mixed reviews and unpopular refurbishments, one thing has always remained a constant: Disney Adult's love for the purple dragon. Yet things really escalated when it was reported that EPCOT guests were queuing between 2 and 7 hours to get their hands on a Figment popcorn bucket. This was one of the longest wait times in Walt Disney World history!

You better believe this isn't where the dedication stops. Every year, there are always queues outside of The Emporium, the souvenir shop on Main Street USA in Magic Kingdom, for the Halloween merch at Mickey's Not-So-Scary Halloween Party. Though the queues will go down throughout the evening as more events happen, people still scramble to be amongst the first to purchase that year's new line of merchandise.

Situations like this happen at all the Disney Parks worldwide, which only highlights the commitment and dedication of Disney fans. Many of the people who queue up are content creators who share images of the merch online. The fact that there are people out there hungry for that content shows how much people love Disney products. Don't even get me started on the queues for Walt Disney World's 50th anniversary.

I understand that this is a huge part of commercialisation, and for Disney to increase their revenue, which you can't really fault, it's a brilliant move. But I also love that this community of people who create their own artwork can share their passion with other Disney lovers has come from here.

I adore the fact that I can walk onto the absolutely abhorrent Bakerloo line, and amongst the heaving crowd, I can immediately spot a lounge fly. Without even conversing with that person, I know we share something in common: A large credit card bill and a fierce love for Disney.

Due to the growth in the merchandise, it's very easy to spot a Disney Adult. You better believe that if I see someone with a Mickey antenna topper trying to pull out onto a busy road, I'm going to literally stop traffic to let them out.

Whether you like Disney or not, you're never going to be able to get away from it. Wherever you go, there's going to be a little bit of Disney magic somewhere: on a key ring, on a T-shirt, or me dragging a giant-sized Mickey teddy down the street. Disney has found a way to become ever-present in our world, and that is something I truly celebrate. World domination? We're getting there, guys.

Lydia's favourite Disney Villains

1. Hades. Come on, it goes without saying.
2. Yzma.
3. Cruella de Vil, she's sassy af, and I respect that.
4. Gaston. And not just because he's sexy.
5. Ursula.
6. Syndrome. I would also dedicate my life to being just that petty.
7. Hans, I'm just not over that plot twist, ok?
8. Lots'-o-Huggin' Bear. I also thought it was just spelt Lotso. Either way, he is one sadistic bear.
9. Dr Facilier.
10. Mother Gothel. Not a big fan of the whole kidnapping children thing, but she's a vibe.

Step 5: Eat a Mickey Shaped Diet

When you travel anywhere, a huge part of immersing yourself in that culture is eating the food. Disney Parks has developed its own much-loved cuisine, which people (me included) can't wait to smash their faces into.

When it comes to the menus of any European or American theme park, the first dishes that come to mind are things like hot dogs and candyfloss. Disney Parks are no exception in this culture. However, over the years, they have developed this to a whole new level. You can still get your sausages and fluffy sugar throughout the parks, but it has expanded far beyond the basics.

So, when you adopt a Disney Adult, how do you know what to feed it? Well, Disney Adults have six food groups: frozen treats, sweet treats, plastic cheese, themed meals, coffee, and absolutely anything Mickey-shaped.

This might all feel quite self-explanatory, but if this is your first time feeding a Disney Adult, for their sake and yours, I don't want you to get this wrong. So I am, of course, going to break this down for you.

Frozen treats. And I'm not talking about sucking off Olaf. Ice cream is one of the most popular treats known to human beings. Primarily recognised as an indulgent way to drown your sorrows, yet when it comes to Disney ice cream, there sure aren't any sorrows.

In recent years, Dole Whips have become the most iconic frozen snack at Disney World, even rivalling anything Mickey-shaped. For those who don't know, a Dole Whip is, most simply, a pineapple soft serve. It can be served either in a cup on its own or as a float in pineapple juice.

The origin of Dole Whips at Disney dates back to 1986 when the first one was sold at the Enchanted Tiki Room's Tiki Juice Bar in Disneyland. The company Dole became an official sponsor, and soon after, it began appearing at Walt Disney World. Since then, Dole Whips have been popping up all over the parks and have evolved into many different forms and specials.

Dole Whips are no longer limited to pineapple; they're now available in an array of different flavours. However, it must be noted that this varies depending on the park, the kiosk, the season, and what specials are currently running (these change constantly). We've seen character-themed floats like Moana, ride-themed floats like Jungle Cruise and alcoholic floats (fuck yeah).

Although possibly the most popular, these aren't the only frozen treats you can get at Disney. Soft serve ice cream, commonly mixed up **with** Dole Whips, is popular for its speciality cones, which pop up all over Disney Parks and are regularly changed.

An example of this is in 2022, Storybook Treats in Fantasyland ran a series of Seven Dwarves cones themed to the different dwarves. Over the months, they changed between the famous seven and were different in flavour and design. Although a Sneezy ice cream doesn't sound all that appealing, he certainly wasn't overlooked.

The Dole Whip's ultimate competition has to be the Mickey Premium bar, another very iconic treat in the parks. These can be bought from almost any cart, and although they appear to simply be a Mickey-shaped choc ice, this magical treat truly completes a day in the parks.

The bars have remained relatively consistent over the years, although the packaging has changed slightly. They have become so popular that it's even possible to buy them by the box from some stores in America. If you're ever lucky enough to go on a Disney Cruise, you'll find that you can have an unlimited supply of bars completely free of charge during your trip.

The iced treats don't stop there; there are sundaes, ice cream sandwiches, slushies, iced coffee, milkshakes, you name it, Disney has thought of it. And don't even get me started on the kitchen sink.

I think due to the warm climate of many of the Disney Parks around the world, having something cold to cool you down after a long, sweltering day on your feet is just all the more special. But remember to eat it fast because not only will it melt, but Disney Adults will also bite.

Now that we've covered the frozen treats, what about all the other temperature treats? I'm generally not a sweet tooth, but that all goes out the window the minute that I have a castle on my peripheral. Wherever you go in the world, people love to hunt down the best sweet treats, and with Disney, you don't have to do all that much hunting.

There are the obvious treats that people will go for, like cupcakes and cookies. But Disney takes this to the next level with both the flavours and the theming. Popular examples include The Grey Stuff Cupcake from Gaston's Tavern, which people can't wait to get their hands on. The Cheshire Cat Tail is available on both Main Street and Fantasyland. The Wookie Cookie from Galaxy's Edge. All of these items are popular because not only are they fun, but they're also so tasty.

Other popular sweet treats at Disney include Mickey beignets, which encourage many Disney Adults to beeline for Port Orleans resorts since that was, until recently, the only place you could get them in Walt Disney World. Hopefully, their residence in Magic Kingdom will be permanent, and we'll have easy access to those white powdered delights. I'm talking about the sugar, by the way.

Mickey waffles are always available at breakfast dining, but they're also available from specific quick-service dining sites throughout the parks. They come with different toppings and are served alongside other popular waffle dishes.

School bread, caramel popcorn, Jack Jack's cookie, macarons, brioche, cronuts, wonuts, donuts. Fuck me, I need to check my blood sugar just writing this post. And nowhere else in the world would you find me getting a return time, then waiting in a queue for a bastard cookie. But for Gideon's, I would do just about anything.

Every time I have a trip coming up, Disney Food Blog and I become best friends. I keep up to date with the new incoming treats and begin making my snack wish list. But in reality, it's not a treat; it's an essential part of Disney Adulting. How else would I have the energy to yeet the kids out the way during rope drop?

If I wouldn't be swiftly imprisoned by the local law enforcement for walking around a Disney park with a needle in my arm, I would absolutely be attached to an IV of plastic cheese during my trips. I dream about smearing that gooey orange cheese all over my body and...

I'm sorry. I got a bit caught up there. But it should come as no surprise to any Disney Adult that plastic cheese should be on the list. Despite its less-than-appetising name, this cheese has become a classic at Disney Parks, and everyone is desperate to get a pretzel or corn dog nuggets so that they can get a side of that liquid gold.

Although it is of the utmost importance to keep a Disney Adult topped up with a constant supply of plastic cheese, there is a wealth of other savoury snacks that will also do the trick. A fan-favourite and a big love of mine are the spring rolls from the cart near Adventureland. These rose in popularity after Tim Tracker, a YouTube vlogger, shared his love for them many years ago. Since then, people have flocked to try the ever-popular cheeseburger spring rolls and the other flavours they transition in.

As we know, popcorn is always a popular choice at Disney. Although sweet options are more commonly selected, salty options are available, including a unique variant at Galaxy's Edge. At Kat Saka's Kettle, guests can buy the Outpost Popcorn Mix, which is a mix of colourful, savoury popcorn with spicy seasoning.

Loaded fries & tots are always a favourite theme park option. These are available all over the Disney Parks and in different flavours. Animal Kingdom even offers a stand where you can mix and match your sauces. You could even pull out your IV and give them a squirt of cheese.

EPCOT's World Showcase offers a maze of different cuisines. Eating around the world has become a popular activity among Disney Adults, where you get a snack or food item from every nation. I love to do this during the festivals when they have special pop-ups and booths with unique food items you can't get during other seasons.

This means I can walk along and have pasta from Italy, and then at the next moment, I can have a bratwurst from Germany. You'll never see a Disney Adult bouncier than taking in all the foods of the world at EPCOT. But that could be the alcohol, too.

An always controversial choice: the Turkey Leg. Many online debates centre around this famous snack. Whether you love it or hate it, it has become a staple of Disney snacking. It may not be a favourite of mine, but if it gets your Disney blood pumping, who am I to judge?

Disney isn't all about grabbing food in boxes and eating on trash cans. As unglamorous as it sounds, it's a major part of the process. But every now and again, a Disney Adult has to pick up metal cutlery, leave the IV at the door, and sit down at a table.

Table-service dining is a great part of the Disney experience. Sometimes, it can be hard to tear yourself away from the hustle and bustle of the attractions, but you don't realise how much good it can do you to separate your ankles from the strollers for a brief period.

Table service restaurants are available at all Disney Parks all over the world. However, since Walt Disney World is the biggest and most familiar resort, it's going to be the one I focus on more as an example. Some Disney restaurants you can just walk into, be seated, and eat. However, due to the popularity of a lot of the restaurants, just like the outside world, you have to book in advance.

Bring on the ADRs. As you probably know by now, Disney involves a lot more planning than your usual, 'what time should we put our towel on the sunbed?' kind of holiday. Dining is no exception. ADRs, otherwise known as Advance Dining Reservations, are where you book your dining in advance of your holiday. There are over 100 sit-down restaurants at Disney World, so as you can imagine, it is going to take a little bit of research to find your preferences.

If you have taken on board the newly returned Disney Dining Plan, where you pay for tokens that you exchange for meals. Then you may have to do a lot more booking if you have the Table Service Dining credits. This is because you're probably going to be doing at least one of these a day. If you're going without the plan, which became the more popular option while we waited on the return of free Disney Dining, then you might be a bit more selective about when and where you eat.

Whether you're staying on-site at Disney or not, you can make ADRs 60 days before the day you want to visit the restaurant. However, if you're staying at a Disney Resort, you can make the reservations for your entire trip 60 days before the first day of your trip. Are you still with me, guys? This shit is like a fucking law degree.

So, if you're booking for your entire trip, you're going to want to start with the days with the most in-demand restaurants like Be Our Guest or Cinderella's Royal Table, then work down your list. Dining opens at 6:00 am EST, which is 11:00 am in the UK. So if you're like me and aren't fucking about, you're going to treat this like Renaissance Tour tickets and have the My Disney Experience App open and loaded long before they go live.

Have your credit card at the ready, as the restaurant will hold it and charge you if you don't appear for the reservation. A top tip here is to have your card information already input into the My Disney Experience App so that it does this automatically. I told you, I'm not fucking about here.

Reservations can be cancelled up to 2 hours in advance, which gives you plenty of time to change your mind. It also gives you a chance to snag last-minute reservations. If you had your heart set on one meal and couldn't quite get it? Don't worry; keep checking the app, as cancellations pop up all the time. Disney Adults even go as far as to join reservation Facebook groups where people post if they're going to cancel a booking; this gives someone a chance to get straight on there and snatch it up.

This level of strategy when planning is one of the most significant parts Disney Adults love. Some people don't mind going with the flow and just hoping for the best, which honestly does work. But those who are crazy like me will have six different live spreadsheets on what restaurants they want to go to in priority order.

You can dine in a T-Rex, in Belle's Ballroom, have a BBQ with Woody & friends, eat seafood in a boat, have breakfast with Stitch or even dine in Cinderella's castle. There is so much to offer in terms of Disney Dining, and what's the point in having a meal if Mickey isn't going to come and hug you at your table? Wasted calories, if not.

That was an extremely fucking complex food group. You know what isn't complicated? Coffee. And Jesus Christ, a Disney Adult needs it. You're telling me you got through the ADR paragraph without caffeine?

Going to a Disney park is exhausting. You might be travelling with kids or just trying to get Lydia to stop having a panic attack over her dining reservations. However you're doing it, you're going to need coffee.

Whichever park you're going to, you will find a Starbys. And I bet you my plastic cheese drip that before 10 am, it's one of the longest queues in the park. Don't let that deter you; rope-dropping cannot be done without coffee, and luckily, Starbucks isn't your only option.

Joffrey's is the official speciality coffee of Walt Disney World and Disneyland. Not only will you find it being sold at stands throughout the parks, but you can also buy it by bag in souvenir shops. So if anyone ever hears me say 'let's get a bag in' at Disney World, that's precisely what I'm talking about. Swears. I don't know what it is about this coffee, whether it is actually nice or it's just another contributor to my Disney addiction, but I'm obsessed with it.

If you stay on-site at one of the Disney Resorts, Mousekeeping will leave Joffrey's pods/ coffee bags for you to use on the machines in your room. Nothing gets me out of bed at 5 am, ready to get in a virtual queue, quite like a Disney coffee in my Disney room. You can also buy it at the quick-service counters at your resort if you want to take it with you on the transport to the parks. Even better, you can put it in your resort mug as part of the price.

Whether you're going to drink it in your room, bring it from home, buy it in the parks, or set up another IV, you're going to need coffee to get you through your Disney day. I never even bother to add it to my snack wishlist, because I already know that a good portion of my food budget, some of my t-shirt budget, and my gas & electric budget for the following month is going to be spent on Joffrey's coffee. If you ever see a Disney Adult curled up in a ball, shaking on the side of Main Street, just sprinkle some pixie dust (coffee beans) over them and watch them fly.

The final food group, and probably the most essential of them all, is any and all food Mickey-shaped. It is perhaps a surprise to non-Disney Adults that you can find food at Disney that isn't in the shape of our favourite mouse. Yet there are still a hell of a lot of options that are.

You better believe it isn't a Disney trip until I've rammed those 3 circles in my mouth. This doesn't happen anywhere else, as I usually just stick to the 2 balls. I'm not even smoking a cigarette at Disney unless it's Mickey-shaped.

Ice cream bars, pretzels, beignets, waffles, ice cream sandwiches, cake pops, rice krispie treats, candy apples, cinnamon rolls, mousse, and cookies. Whichever form it takes, every Disney Adult's sole food intake needs to be in the shape of Mickey.

You're probably noticing a bit of a theme here that this is slightly fixating on the American parks; this is because they're more familiar to me. However, I know that wherever in the world you choose to visit Disney, there is a vast selection of amazing treats awaiting you.

The food at Disney is one of the most enjoyable parts of the parks. As I said, it's way more than just hot dogs and cotton candy. The food is a massive part of the experience, and trust me, you're going to love it.

A balanced diet is vital for a healthy life as a Disney Adult, so these food groups should be taken very seriously. So whether you've just finished a Mickey premium bar, are about to have one, or are counting down to your next. Let's tap our chocolate-covered Mickey and say cheers to the fucking ears.

Lydia's Favourite Disney Snacks

1. Grand Marnier Slushie.
2. Just about anything else alcoholic.
3. Cheeseburger Spring Rolls.
4. Mickey red velvet cake pop.
5. Ronto Wrap.
6. Everything dipped in plastic cheese.
7. Themed Soft Serves.
8. Mickey Beignets.
9. Night Blossom drink.
10. Mickey Waffles (the best with the Ohana's breakfast).

Step 6: Do all The Crazy

I've spent **the** last few chapters talking about the fundamentals of being a Disney Adult. Although these are what make up the bottom of the pyramid, that still doesn't necessarily make you a Disney Adult. No, as a Disney Adult, you have to take this shit next level. Starve your wedding guests for the sake of Disney. Breakdown in front of the castle. Wrestle the childless millennial haters to the floor.

It's these acts that have allowed Disney Adults to earn their title. So, am I asking you to go out and start having fights with people on Main Street? Yes, destroy them all.

No, I'm kidding. For the love of all things Disney, do not actually do that. That's a one-way ticket to a lifetime ban, and nothing is going to keep a Disney Adult up at night quite like the concept of existence with no Disney eVer, eer agai n.

Sorry, I'm literally shaking as I write that.

So, how do we level up? What takes us from a person who just enjoys a Disney film to being a Disney Adult? A typical fan would say they regularly see new movies and visit a park or 2 when they can. Disney Adults, on the other hand? Well, let's Mama Odie this shit and dig a little deeper.

Though the negative connotations surrounding the term Disney Adults have only recently emerged, the way I see it,

Disney Adults is the title for the fandom. In the same way, you have Beyhive, Cumberbitches, Whovians, Potterheads, Beliebers, Gooners, Directioners, Swifties, Barmy Army, and so many more.

D23, which I will discuss more in a later chapter, is the official fan club. Yet, in recent times, Disney Adults has been the more appropriate term for the fandom since it is a subculture composed of those who share a love for Disney. I also think that by taking it in as our own, we take control over the term, and it can no longer be negative.

Throughout history, we have seen different fandoms receive hate for various reasons. Usually, it is a lack of understanding or jealousy over the passion and community the fandom shares. Disney has, of course, been no exception to this. Yet, more recently, it has reached the height of its unpopularity.

Why this may be runs a lot deeper than just a general dislike for Disney. I consider myself to be a nerd, a term I wear proudly. This term has also garnered negative undertones through the years. Yet I only see the positive side of it: that I am devoted to something that I enjoy and that I am knowledgeable about— something I have never and will never see as a bad thing.

I would say I'm a part of a few different fandoms, but Disney is one I hold all the more closely, not only because of what it means to me but also because I feel a need to protect it. I know this book will feel very fixated on the dislike Disney Adults receive, but for a hot second, I want to ignore the hate. I want to celebrate all those who are unapologetically Disney Adults.

If you own a wall full of Disney ears, I fucking applaud you. You're telling me you're going to Disney 3 times this year? Good for you. Did you watch A Bug's Life twice this week? I understand. These are all the things that make up who you are

69

as a Disney Adult, and you should be proud of them.

Those who don't like Disney in my office have quickly come to despise me. That's because whenever I get hold of the Bluetooth speaker, you better believe that Disney music is going on. But we all know the classics, right? If Circle of Life comes on, there are going to be very few people in the room who don't recognise it.

However, I didn't realise how familiar I was with Disney music until we started playing entire soundtracks. I quickly learned that within a few seconds of Disney scores being played, like Nemo's Egg, Vuelie, Transformation, etc., I could identify which film they came from almost instantly. I've listened to Son of a Man so many damn times that when I hear someone about to sneeze, I think it's the start of the song.

Ok, Lydia, that's fair enough; you're a total film nerd, so that's to be expected. Alright, I hear you. I'll let you have that one. Let's take it up a notch. It quickly transpired that I could name secondary characters from a quick photo, tell you what Disney Park a ride lives in, and speak in Disney acronyms like it's an entirely different language.

I haven't learned these things by making notes from books like I'm revising for a test. I've absorbed them over the years of being immersed in the Disney universe. I watch the films frequently, follow all the Disney pages, keep up to date with the news, and live on Disney Tok.

Owning the merchandise and visiting the parks are part of being a Disney Adult, but they aren't what define you. I've seen online people say that they can't categorise themselves as Disney Adults because they can't afford those things, they don't have the time to visit the parks, or they don't have the space to keep the stuff.

That doesn't mean you should be locked out of the fandom I'm telling the guards to open up the fucking gates because, guys, you have just as much of a right to be here as the next Loungefly hoarder.

Being a Disney Adult is as much a state of mind as a physical practise. If you want to be in the gang, come and sit next to your best friend Lydia and let's talk about how you feel about the re-theming of the defunct Dinoland USA. However, one of the biggest takeaways I want people to get from this book is that Disney Adults are crazy. I am totally fucking bonkers. But there is nothing wrong with that.

I've had lengthy discussions with my cousin over which bathrooms are the best at Magic Kingdom. I've fallen so deep into my love for Disney that I've convinced myself it is socially acceptable to talk about fucking bathrooms. It's the Tangled ones, by the way.

But I'm actually not the only one. There are articles, YouTube videos, and online discussions literally breaking down this very topic. I wasn't the first person to think this was a worthy subject of conversation, and I sure as shit won't be the last.

It's not unusual for Disney Adults to get excited over rare things at Disney. I mentioned previously how trash cans at Disney have their own groupies. It's got to the point where you can buy smaller copies of the Disney trash cans to have in your house. This is how far Disney Adults will go with their merchandise. Buying bins. And you better believe I'm about to order one.

Disney Adults also brought about the love for Disney walls. Now, if you're a Disney Adult, you've got to know about the obsession with Disney walls. Fans started hunting down their favourite painted walls at Disney Parks and sharing photos with them. Popular ones include the purple wall in Tomorrowland in Magic Kingdom and the bubblegum wall at EPCOT.

They've accumulated such a fan base that merchandise has been created from them, mainly from small independent businesses, aka Disney Adults. But Disney can't pretend that their lilac merchandise range wasn't somewhat inspired by that famed wall.

One of the only things that separates the adults from the children at Disney Parks is that adults aren't allowed to dress up in costume. This, I believe, is fair as it takes the magic away from the actual meet-and-greets. However, Disney Adults have found their own way around this rule through the art of Disney Bounding.

Disney Adults will dress in outfits similar in colour or style to that of a Disney character so that they represent them without directly replicating their outfit. This has become an enjoyable way for people to express themselves and is another thing I love about Disney Adults. Instead of going, 'WTF Disney, why are you stopping us from dressing up?', they just went, 'No worries, hun. We hear you, we'll work out our own thing!'

Even outside of this, Disney Adults weren't going to let it go. I had to get that in somewhere, guys. Give me a break. They embrace costumes at Halloween, outside of the parks at D23 or other events where they can cosplay. I love how seriously people take this. Some of the costumes are honestly amazing. I swear, it's the most interested I've ever been in partaking in role-play. And you know exactly what I mean.

This is a side of being a Disney Adult that is harmless, wholesome fun, but that inevitably isn't where it stops. There are then the Disney Adults who take it to a whole other level, and I've got to admit I find it unbelievably entertaining. You might think the concept of being a Disney Adult is a relatively new phenomenon, but that couldn't be further from the truth.

Back in 1998, when it was rumoured that Disney was to close Mr Toad's Wild Ride, dedicated fans flocked to the ride to picket and protest its closure. The movement garnered a lot of interest from dedicated 'Toadies', and many people turned up with banners and T-shirts to try and save the cherished ride.

This isn't the only time this has happened; once again, fans became very protective of the 'Take Flight / Delta Dreamflight' attraction in Tomorrowland, which was replaced with Buzz Lightyear's Space Ranger Spin. Of course, these are all things of the past. Buzz Lightyear and The Many Adventures of Winnie the Pooh have grown to be loved by Disney fans. But you can't help but admire the lengths Disney Adults were willing to go to protect the traditional rides.

Similar situations have happened more recently when fans heard rumours of closures and jumped in to save the attraction. It became widely believed that The Carousel of Progress was going to be shut down and replaced, which hardcore Disney World fans weren't going to have. After much online campaigning, attendance at this attraction surged. It's unknown if this is the reason that the replacement never happened, but either way, it's still standing strong now!

Though it's more in the online world that we now witness these protests, there have been times when they have found success. The popular Happily Ever After firework show was replaced by Enchantment for the 50th Anniversary of Walt Disney World. With it came a major uproar from the fans of the original show. And I can't lie; I was sharpening my pitchfork. Happily Ever After is one of my favourite things about Walt Disney World. I watch it on YouTube pretty much every week.

I did enjoy Enchantment, but it didn't quite slap for me like HEA did. It turned out that a lot of people shared my opinion, and people started hounding Disney to bring back the nighttime show. And lo and behold, Disney obliged! It was announced at D23 in 2022 that the much-adored show was making its grand return to Magic Kingdom, and the fans couldn't have been happier.

I love that the fans literally bullied Disney into bringing it back, kind of like when the internet bullied Kylie Jenner into changing her son's name. A big round of applause to Disney, though. They listened to their fans and gave them what they wanted. You have to commend them for that.

Disney Adults have naturally taken this to a much darker place. Some park guests have even gone as far as to dump ashes in the park despite the strict rules against doing so. Not only will the remains end up in waste disposal, but a gust of wind could seriously darken what would've been a lovely family photo in front of the castle.

The rules are in place for safety and respect. However, there are those who still in spite of this, go ahead with it anyway. So next time you're on Pirates, smelling that oh, so beautiful Pirates of the Caribbean smell, maybe be careful how hard you inhale. Especially if you see something questionable floating alongside the boat. You could end up snorting a fat line of someone's great Aunt Debra. Now that's a souvenir.

Just like in ordinary, non-Disney life, demise is a bit of a fascination for a few people. Disney World is no exception. Some fans have become fixated on deaths that have occurred in the Disney Parks, albeit from rides, negligence, or natural causes. There is even a book by a Cast Member called 'The Park After Dark', which breaks down these tragic occurrences and discusses Disney Park's ghosts. They're a thing, guys. Just look up George and the Pirates of the Caribbean ride.

If you think that's dark, I'm going to take you back to 2013 Disney was forced to intervene after it became public knowledge that families were hiring wheelchair-bound tour guides to pose as family members in order to be able to skip queues. Now, as highly inappropriate as this is, you can't help but admire the ingenious slightly. And these guides were earning some serious cash. As soon as the black market guides became public knowledge, the operation was swiftly shut down. So don't go get any ideas, guys.

Another reason Disney Adults are regularly attacked is people's desire to go to a Disney Park for their honeymoon. Now, I, of course, don't see any problem with this. But it comes as no surprise that people get seriously aggravated, claiming it's going too far to want to spend your honeymoon as a newlywed at a Disney Park.

I can see why some people might take it in this direction. It's not exactly a secret that a honeymoon is about love, romance and good, old-fashioned, dirty sex. Why would a couple want to be doing that at a Disney resort? There are those online who have even resorted to accusing these people of having perverted intentions and that their internet history should be checked.

Now, I'm not going to lie to you; those comments made me howl. Of course, it isn't true, but you've got to laugh. As for sex in a Disney resort? Well, that's just found its way onto my bucket list. But please leave my internet history alone.

The problem with situations like this, and to be honest with most of them in life, is people always have to take things a teeny bit too seriously. An example of this is people getting irate about the sexualisation of Disney. Because so many believe Disney is exclusively for children, they disagree with associating it with adult-related things. I completely agree with this, being the moral citizen that I am. Why anyone would ever want to sexualise a Disney character is beyond me. There's just no line any more. Fucking perverts.

When it comes to Disney Adults, it's not all perversion and human remains. There are far more warm and virtuous ways that Disney Adults display their passion, such as creating their own traditions. There are so many things that have become a part of Walt Disney World and the community that the Disney company has nothing to do with.

Gifting to Cast Members to show their appreciation and leaving notes or treats for Mousekeeping are both lovely examples of fan-generated practises that are independent of Disney. They have now become widely acknowledged by guests, and many take them on themselves.

I've also seen guests wanting to share their own magic around the parks, leaving notes and presents for other guests to find. I can't think of a greater example of how cute Disney Adults really can be.

Back in 2021, a photo went viral of a father cropping out his daughter in a selfie with Buzz Lightyear and Woody at the Disney Parks. Everyone loved the humour of this man taking his moment with the characters while his daughter stood and watched. Of course, this man didn't neglect his daughter; she had her moment with many other characters. But as a lifelong Toy Story fan, this man just got so excited that he couldn't stop himself from jumping in for a photo.

His girlfriend snapped the hilarious moment, and the internet loved it. No one was going at him for bad parenting or any of that stupid bullshit. Instead, they laughed along and celebrated the fact that this man was enjoying his moment too. The thing is, although he went there to take his daughter to Disney, it was his trip as well.

Adults have just as much of a right to enjoy Disney as children do. And yes, we are a little bit crazy, but at least you'll never see me throw myself on the floor having a tantrum because I can't get a Mickey Premium bar—not often, anyway.

So be crazy and stand up for what you believe in. Hey, it worked for Happily Ever After! Why can't we all just enjoy Disney together? Adults, children, and your late Great Aunt Debra. All for one and one for all.

Times Lydia has cried about Disney

1. When I saw that video of the 2 toddlers wearing a Slinky Dog costume.
2. Seeing Cinderella's Castle for the first time as an adult. Cue 'What Dreams Are Made Of.'
3. Every single time I've ever seen Happily Ever After.
4. My second speeding ticket in a week, and I realised I might have to half my Disney snack budget.
5. Anything Make a Wish.
6. When 'Go the Distance' came on in World of Disney while I was buying my first spirit jersey.
7. All of the Disney 100 promos on social media, especially the 'You helped make this dream come true' one. I played that at least 10 times a day for a good week.
8. Any time a character in the parks does sign language.
9. When I surpassed 18-years-old and realised I had to start funding my own Disney trips.
10. When someone read my Disney blog and told me I should write a book.

Step 7: Protect the Cast Members

The big man himself, Walt Disney, proudly stated that 'it takes people to make the dream a reality'. Disney Cast members have always been at the heart of what makes the Disney Parks what they are. There is without doubt magic at the parks, but it's the Cast Members who make it.

In case you're new to the term, a Disney Cast Member refers to any employee of a Disney Park or Disney Store. The title has been used since Disneyland's opening back in 1955.

Walt wanted the magic to start for his guests the minute they stepped foot in the parks, and he was relying on his Cast Members to do this. For him, that was when the 'show started', and it was the employees who put on this show.

Anytime a Cast Member can be seen by, or comes in contact with park guests, they are regarded as 'on-stage.' Walt always used theatrical terminology when it came to his parks to help emphasise the 'show' feel. Cast Members don't wear uniforms; instead, they wear costumes, and they all undergo in-depth training on how to behave in front of the guests.

Anytime a Cast Member is off-stage, this means they're working on what is going on behind the scenes and aren't witnessed by the guests. This helped shape the mystery of how the park comes to life. The process of coming 'on-stage' and 'off-stage' is a seamless procedure and is managed and directed by stage professionals.

Therefore, whenever you're interacting with a Cast Member, they're always in character. They're taught to keep a positive, family-friendly atmosphere and show kindness to guests. I salute this because I swear to god, if I had kids coming up and prodding me all day, an eff and a jeff would slip out on more than one occasion.

The recruitment process for a Disney Cast Member is also very different from that for an ordinary job. Although interviews and CVs will be included, for the more speciality roles like performing and portraying characters, an extensive audition process takes place. This is not only to look for similarities in appearance to the characters but also to see if you have the skills to fit the role.

Whether you're going to be friends with Snow White or taking photos of guests with her, all Cast Members undergo comprehensive training. This includes a Disney Traditions class, area-specific training, and attraction training. At the core of it all is an emphasis on making an emotional connection with guests.

Despite the training that these Cast Members go through, can you be taught to make the magic? I don't think so. There may be just under 40,000 Cast Members working at Walt Disney **World**, but a hell of a lot more people than that applied to work there. I believe these people were selected purely because they could see the potential for them to create magic for the guests.

In Doug Lipp's book Disney U, he describes how the leader of Disney University would get heavily involved in the Cast Member experience. They would regularly have open conversations and take feedback, proving their commitment to promoting an enjoyable work environment. It's no secret to anyone on the corporate ladder that happy employees make for a more successful business. This is something that Disney strives to achieve.

I know there is some debate over the experience of working at the Disney Parks. It can be arduous manual labour, along with long hours. Despite that, all I ever see on TikTok from Cast Members who land a position is them celebrating getting their dream job. There aren't many other lines of work where I see such an overwhelmingly positive reaction to employment.

Many people dream of landing a role as a Disney character. One aspect of these meet-and-greets I love is how Disney focuses more on teaching an actor how to interact with guests than on their portrayal of the character. Disney recognises that it is so much more about the exchange than the believability that they are the actual characters.

Despite that, Disney works hard not to break down the illusion of the characters, even going as far as requesting employees not to say that they play a particular character, and instead that they're friends with them. If children start hearing the actors saying things like I'm Snow White, or I play Snow White, it will ruin the magic for them. By Cast Members saying they're friends with that character, they still get to talk about their experience in the role without spoiling the magic.

Before Cast Members learn anything about their role as characters or any other position in the park, they have to go through training about the company's history. By learning about the journey of the Disney company, they understand the values on a deeper level. This also keeps Walt's vision and memory alive by encouraging employees to follow his ethos, which is honestly one of the loveliest tributes they could do for him.

Disney's treatment of Cast Members is regularly discussed online. In the same way, every major corporation comes under scrutiny and should strive to improve conditions. However, when you delve deep into the opportunities that Disney creates for Cast Members, it's pretty impressive. We must understand more about Cast Members and their experiences in order to genuinely appreciate them.

Let's start with the Disney College Program, something I deeply regret not doing. I can't believe after tens of thousands of pounds doing the most pointless degree in the world, I didn't even take advantage and have a summer in Disney. Bullshit. But for those who are more intelligent than me, this scheme is fantastic for university students who want to spend a summer in Walt Disney World.

Anyone enrolled in a university course can apply and then spend the season living, working and experiencing Walt Disney World with a community of other college students. This not only gives students a chance to live and work internationally but also meet people from all over the world. Not to mention, you get free entry to the Disney Parks on your days off. Why 21-year-old Lydia was boozing in the local pub and not in EPCOT is beyond me.

The Disney Aspire Program invests in Disney Employees and their education by offering them opportunities to meet their academic goals. This can take the form of paying for tuition, reimbursing for supplies, or breaking down barriers to higher education. This encourages employees to continue with their education, invest in themselves, and prosper within the Disney company.

I know I sound like a bloody car salesman for the Disney HR

team. However, until I started looking into careers with Disney, I had yet to learn how many opportunities were out there. It makes me super excited for the Cast Members who work so hard for the company. Knowing that there is a chance for them to get something back is a huge perk.

There is also a programme called Disney VoluntEARS, where Cast Members can offer their time and skills to the community. They can also turn their volunteer hours into charitable donations with grants from the programme. This is an excellent example of the altruism of Disney Cast Members. I told you, they really do make the magic.

So, other than the programmes, how else do you end up working for Disney? Well, Disney has a careers website where they regularly post available jobs from all around the world; all you need to do is apply. I think one of the biggest things to remember when working for such a big company like Disney is that there are so many different positions you could go for.

When people think of Disney jobs, they mainly think of either dressing up as a character or working at a shop. If you broadened your horizons, you would think of the custodial staff, the security, and the photographers. But this is just the tip of the iceberg.

When Disney+ released its original series 'One Day at Disney Shorts,' it gave viewers an insight into what it is like to work for Disney in all of these different positions. There are now 50 mini episodes, as well as the original hour-long documentary, that follow the day-to-day lives of the various people who work for the company.

From Animators and Actors, all the way to the Seamstresses, Zookeepers, Story Artists, Chocolatiers, Imagineers, and even the big lad Bob Iger himself. There are so many stories about the wildest and most impressive positions at Disney. It is so interesting to think about the positions you just never would've thought about, like Thom Self, the Mechanist and Scuba Diver for the Finding Nemo Submarine Voyage at Disneyland.

It never even occurred to me that you would need someone for that role. This just shows how many positions there are for so many different people with different skill sets. It also puts into context the level of talent required to make not only Disney Parks function, but the company as a whole.

This is why I will always protect Cast Members from literally anything. I would throw my sister in front of a car just to protect some random guy who drew Mickey on the pavement with water during my last trip. I don't even know what your name is, but I got you, good sir.

It is clear that Cast Members go through a lot to bring the Disney Parks to life, with training, long hours, and hard work in all weather conditions. Some people may argue that it's a paying job in the most magical place on earth, so why should we applaud them for that? Because it doesn't stop there.

Disney Cast Members go above and beyond for guests every single day at the parks. Anyone who has been lucky enough to visit will be able to recall at least one moment when they experienced the magic of a Cast Member.

If you look through Disney Park fan pages on social media, there is a wealth of examples of how Cast Members have gone the extra mile to make guests' experiences a little bit more magical. Cast Members are allowed to give out extra surprises and treats to guests during the work day. Many fans refer to this as being 'pixie-dusted'. This happens in many different ways. Sometimes, it's being allowed to ride an attraction a second time without queuing, getting an extra snack, or being chosen to take part in a special activity.

Sometimes, you can ask Cast Members for these treats, and they will oblige; other times, they will do them without any prompting at all. However, when it happens, it really makes your day a little bit more special.

I've had many amazing experiences like this, from a photo pass photographer who took some time out of her day to follow us around and take candid photos of us without noticing, to a resort pool lifeguard who kept the pool open a little bit later for us and let us ride down the children's slides. Usually, it is the most minor things that can mean the most.

Cast members are also great at calming down scared children or even scared Lydias. A few attractions at Disney can be daunting to children or, again, Lydias, and Cast Members will do their best to calm the child (Lydia) down and explain the ride to them.

I remember reading a story about a lady who was scared to ride a dark ride, but her daughter wanted to go on it. So, the Cast Member took the little girl on the ride herself so she wouldn't miss out. As if that wasn't enough, she then took the time to speak to the mum and comfort her, then took her past the queue to the front of the ride to ride with them both again.

Ok, fine, I'll tell you about my story of when I nearly wimped out. Something you may remember from earlier in the book is I'm an absolute pussy when it comes to riding rollercoasters. I'm a professional bag holder and photo taker when it comes to going on the big rides at Disney. However, on our last trip, Beth had somehow managed to persuade me to get to the front of the Tower of Terror queue.

Despite the other guests riding with us being super patient and reassuring, at the last minute, I bolted and ran to the lift that takes you back down at a more respectable and humane speed. As I stood there shaking, frustrated with myself for being such a coward, the Cast Member halted the ride and came over to talk me through it. She was so lovely and comforting that she managed to persuade me to go back to the ride.

I walked back into that lift to a roar of applause and cheers. Although I felt as heroic as Captain America when he picked up Mjolnir, it quickly dawned on me that I still had to actually get through the ride. Though it may have been the second worst 4 minutes of my life, my ex being the first, I was so proud of myself for going through with it. I would never have gone on that ride if it hadn't been for the Cast Member, and I was moved by how she took the time to encourage me to face my fears.

Unfortunately, bad things do still happen at Disney. No amount of Pixie Dust can prevent children from dropping Dole Whips or from a souvenir breaking. But Cast Members will always try to right the wrong if they can. If they're able to, they will replace anything that is damaged. This also extends after your trip. If you get home and find your new Disney mug has broken in your bag during the return journey, contact guest services, and they will ship a new one to your home address. Sadly, it would not count if Beth's boyfriend had deliberately thrown it across the floor.

Whether it's a Disney Cast Member or someone serving you outside of Disney, everyone should always show kindness to anyone who is providing a service. It doesn't cost you anything to help pass plates over to a waitress or even give a basic thank you. I know we sometimes encounter people who are having a bad day, and you may feel they're being impolite, but that is all the more reason to show empathy.

However, it has to be noted that you will be hard-pressed to find a Cast Member who doesn't have a smile. Cast Members work really hard, sometimes harder than people you will encounter in the outside world, and despite that, they still do it all with a smile. They are constantly finding ways to improve your day and make your experience better. This is another thing that sets the Disney experience apart from other holidays.

No one is entitled to anything in life, and you shouldn't ever expect too much from someone who is quite literally just there to do a job. But when it comes to Cast Members, they consistently exceed expectations. This is why it is so imperative to treat them with the same respect and kindness that they do to you.

Unfortunately, there have been cases of guest misconduct towards Cast Members. Thankfully, it isn't something that Disney will tolerate, and guests will be asked to leave the park if they ever mistreat a Cast Member. Alas, just like the outside world, there are still cunts at Disney World.

I implore you on your next trip to thank the Cast Members for what they're doing and show appreciation and gratitude for how they're making your Disney trip even better, because they are, even if you don't realise it.

There are other ways you can show your appreciation for Cast Members other than writing a chapter in a book and absolutely fangirling over them. Did you know that on the My Disney Experience app, there is a section where you can fill out a Cast Compliment? If you scroll down on the homepage, you will be able to fill out a form with the Cast Member's name, hometown, and date of interaction, and your thanks will be sent back to them! Imagine having a terrible day at work and then finding out that someone has taken the time to send you a little bit of love.

If you aren't tech-savvy or don't have the app, then don't worry about it! You can leave a Cast Compliment at guest services. This is particularly special as guest services must receive a wealth of complaints throughout the day. Taking the time to share something positive could do a lot to make their day a little bit brighter. There are guest services at all of the parks. However, if you struggle to find them or don't have the energy, which is fair enough after a long day in the parks, you can always call or email them.

Something I love to see is guests pixie-dusting Cast Members. Over the years, this has become increasingly common, as guests recognise their hard work and want to give back. This doesn't have to be anything major, even just a thank you note, but receiving this is a nice way to provide a keepsake to the person and also a reminder that their work is being recognised.

When you encounter Cast Members, you may also recognise the blue legacy badges. This is the highest honour any Cast Member can receive from Disney. Every few years, Disney gives Cast Members and their peers a chance to nominate someone they believe deserves to become a Walt Disney Legacy holder.

Dream, create, and inspire are the three traits of a legacy holder against which the nominees will be measured. Less than 1% of Cast Members hold prestigious titles, so if you ever come across one, take the time to congratulate that person! Trust me, they deserve it.

It's also been nice to see Disney acknowledge Cast Members more often on social media. Earlier this year, they recognised Willie on TikTok. He is a Hollywood Studios Photopass Photographer who was the most complimented Cast Member for two years in a row. Willie's spirit captured the hearts of everyone with his kindness and enthusiasm for his role. Willie, you are literally adorable, and I really hope I get to see you at Disney real soon!

Whichever way you choose to show your appreciation for Cast Members, you must take the time to do so. As a Disney Adult, you have to be able to acknowledge those who have made the thing you love the most so very possible. We all worship the leading man and his mouse, but we have to remember that none of this would've been possible without the people around him. Something Walt himself constantly took the time to recognise.

This is one of the reasons that at Walt Disney World's 50th anniversary, the company took the time to dedicate the achievement to the Cast Members. The Mickey and Minnie Fab 50 character collection sculptures, unveiled at Disney for the anniversary, were dedicated to the Walt Disney World Cast Members of the past, present, and future. A plaque can now be found at Magic Kingdom recognising Cast Members and thanking them for 'making Walt Disney's dream a reality'.

Alongside this, they also invited back the 'Class of 1971', which included the Cast Members who were present on the day of the park's opening. All of them were presented with special name badges and Mickey ears to thank them for their service to the parks.

It was such a moving moment to see Disney recognise the people who have such a special place in our hearts. Cast Members do get perks, such as special events and first access to new attractions. But in the grand scheme of things, there is never enough of a way to say thank you for what they do.

Next time you visit one of the parks or even your local Disney store, remember to take the time to thank the people who keep the magic alive. Us Disney Adults really wouldn't exist without them, and the truth is most of them are Disney

Adults themselves. This isn't quite a plaque, a ceremony or an exclusive look at a ride, but this chapter is dedicated to the Cast Members of the world. I fucking love you.

Lydia's Favourite Disney Songs

1. Go the Distance – Hercules.
2. Son of Man – Tarzan.
3. He Lives in You – The Lion King (Broadway).
4. Part of Your World – The Little Mermaid (2023).
5. How Far I'll Go – Moana.
6. Show Yourself – Frozen 2.
7. Evermore – Beauty and the Beast (2017).
8. On My Way – Brother Bear.
9. The Family Madrigal – Encanto.
10. I2I – A Goofy Movie.

Step 8: Be a Part of the Community

A fandom, at heart, is a community built on a shared love for something. Disney Adults are absolutely no exception to that description. There is only one thing that brings out a stronger emotion than meeting someone who doesn't like Disney, and that's meeting someone who does.

I recently found that I can quite quickly recognise when I've engaged in a conversation with a Disney Adult. We always play it cool initially. Hinting at the fact that we like Disney and then squinting our eyes ever so slightly to prevent them from appearing **too** wide. You casually discuss the parks the same way you would talk about the middle aisle in Aldi. You're cool, calm, collected. Nothing is going to scare them off.

But there will always be something that triggers us, and that's our tell. A person shares their opinion on Beauty and The Beast, and you can almost visibly see our heart rate increase. Before you know it, you're 10 minutes deep into the Disney Renaissance era and how transformational it was for animation. The second someone does that, I know that I've just made a new bestest-ever friend.

It's then likely to be 3 weeks into that conversation before we realise how much time has passed. I've got my 2009 Florida photos up, comparing them with the other person's trip. We're talking Genie+, Bob Iger and Oswald the fucking Lucky Rabbit before it even occurs to us that there is an audience of onlookers who are not quite sure how to describe what they're witnessing.

But that there is precisely what I mean by the Disney community—complete strangers united in their love for something. You see this kind of community everywhere: football games, concerts, cinemas. For one sweeping moment there is nothing strange about a room full of strangers.

This is why it is so baffling that people feel so particularly threatened by the Disney community. I know it has a large fan base, and there is certainly strength in numbers. However, it can't be that much more of a threat than football fans or other film fandoms.

Whether you see us as the enemy or not, the numbers are certainly there, and the online groups show that. I was first introduced to these back in 2017 when I was planning for our 2018 trip. I met someone who told me about an online Facebook group called 'It's Orlando Time' and how much it helped them with the planning of their trip. Naturally, I couldn't resist joining, and there, I found a community of over 200,000 people sharing their tips, advice, and love for trips to WDW in Orlando.

This group was a huge help as a 21-year-old trying to plan a trip to Florida for the first time independently. Any questions I had that the internet wasn't answering, I could pop in there, and the advice would come flooding in. It's one of those times when you truly see the positive side of social media and how there are people out there who want to use it for good.

I've been in the group ever since, and honestly, it feels like therapy. Of course, it's still fantastic for advice, but it's also a place where I can go if I need a bit of Disney comfort. I can read about other people's trips, share stories of my own, and meet like-minded people. And although it royally fucks me off to read that Samantha from Watford is on her way to Heathrow because it's finally 'their turn' while I'm on my way to a 9am meeting; it brings me some comfort to know that although I'll have to listen to Alfred from HR talk about my office conduct again. Blah, blah, blah. Someone else out there is about to have the most magical of days.

I get so addicted to the posts in It's Orlando Time that I'll be sitting there with a cuppa reading a paragraph about something entirely irrelevant to me. I'll get so deep into a post about flying from Dublin, even though I'll probably never fly from there to Orlando. Tips for taking a baby to Disney? Fascinating stuff. And I'll get so invested in people's personal blogs that I'll feel like I've been on the trip with them. And I will forever wish that Chantelle Champs would dress me up in the costumes she dresses her girls up in. I need that shit in adult size.

I love it because they're unfiltered, unpolished, ordinary people sharing their stories. No one gives a fuck about the grammar, whether the photo has a filter on it, or if you've got sweat dripping down your face in a picture. Which you will do most of the time. People just want to read about you having a good time and what your genuine opinion is. I know that I'd much rather read a post from BeckyBlogs slagging her husband off for eating a salad at Disney World than read something someone's been paid to say.

These are real people with real stories and a genuine love for Disney. I've made a lot of good friends from these groups; sadly, there are no Disney sugar daddies as of yet, although I've hinted heavily. But maybe one day.

These groups aren't perfect and just like anything online, there are still trolls that want to cast their magical cuntiness over everything. Don't get me wrong; I love seeing 68-year-old Doris completely go off on a post because she is adamant that Song of the South isn't a single bit racist. At this point, I have the popcorn in the microwave and am waiting with bated breath for it all to kick off.

Sometimes, it's hard for me not to jump on there, ready to be a keyboard warrior and write an essay starting with Dear Doris and ending with white fragility. But if there's anything I've learned over the years, it's to pick your battles. Fortunately, many group admins on these pages work hard to enforce the group rules.

I know, we all hate rules. I certainly do. Do you know how hard it is not to stress post where the fucking fuck is the water fountain in Fantasyland without being banned for a week for my profanity? It's very fuckitty fucking hard.

Despite that, I have a lot of respect for the people who strive to keep these communities positive and free from conflict. We have enough of that crap in the real world. We don't need them in our safe Disney places. Therefore, Disney group admins, I salute you! And... I'm sorry for the swearing.

When I delved deeper into Facebook, I found that there were these kinds of groups by the thousands. People enjoy sharing things with others who they know will understand. I found this in 2018 when we bumped into Tim Tracker in one of the parks. I was so excited because I'd been watching his videos for years and was buzzing to have gotten to meet him in person.

However, when I told my non-Disney Adult friends and family, no one got it. So, I shared the photo on It's Orlando Time and said how excited I was, and immediately, so many people came to the comments to share their joy for me.

Although there are the trolls, I see more often than not how

Disney fans have each other. I saw a post from a girl last year who had dressed up as Powerline Max for Mickey's Not-so-scary Halloween Party. Powerline Max had pulled her up to dance during the parade, and she was so excited to have gotten to have that moment. However, she realised afterwards that she had nothing documenting it.

This girl then went to one of these Facebook groups to ask if anyone had been at the same parade and captured any footage. Within minutes, she was bombarded with videos from onlookers who had captured the interaction from all different angles. Complete strangers were thrilled this girl had gotten her moment and were excited to share it with her. I found this so touching.

There are so many more examples of how people will go the extra mile to help their fellow Disney Adults. I've seen people sharing photos of proposals, using their free time to Photoshop and edit images for strangers, picking up souvenirs for people who didn't manage to get them on their trip.

Life would be boring if we all liked the same things. I have friends who have interests that couldn't be more opposite to mine, and I'm completely okay with that. Yet there is something so comforting about finding those who understand your passions. Suddenly, your world feels a little bit less lonely. And it has never been more crucial for Disney Adults to have this kind of community with the scrutiny that we're currently under. These groups have become like our air raid shelters.

If, like me, your social media algorithms have become totally Disney-fied, then you will see how many profiles and influencers there are out there dedicated to sharing Disney content. You have people who work at Disney, people who live at Disney, and people who go to Disney every day, all constantly sharing photos, reels, blogs, and vlogs about Disney.

I now follow so many Disney news pages, both official and unofficial, that I am likely to find out that a new ride is opening at Disney before the news of an earthquake currently happening in my area.

Many people work in Disney Media, whose jobs are literally to keep the public updated on what's new in the Disney company – new rides, updates, attraction changes, character comebacks, new food items, Bob Iger coming back for the 347437th time. It's now so easy for us Disney Adults to stay informed, and I for one, bloody love it. You're doing God's work, guys.

I also personally love watching Disney vlogs on YouTube. I've never really been that fussed about YouTube and haven't really watched it for anything other than Disney. But you better believe I watch Tim Tracker more religiously than Coronation Street fans watch the soap. And if someone asked me the profound question of whether I would kill one person to save five, I wouldn't unless Adam Hattan was one of the five. That man must be protected at all costs. There are so many Disney vloggers out there, and many have a high viewership. This puts into context not only how many Disney Adults there are out there but also how there is a hunger for constant Disney content.

Beth and I always watch lots of YouTube videos during the build-up to a Disney trip. I find that it gets me in the Disney mood and hypes me up. We'll watch vlogs, Disney planning videos, park walkthroughs, ride POVs, literally anything. I've had friends walk in on me while sitting and watching a Thunder Mountain POV video. They were like, 'What the hell are you doing? Why are you just watching a ride?' I don't know why it freaked them out so much. There are much worse videos they ould've walked in on me watching.

But this got me thinking about how there is no other type of holiday where you would sit and watch videos about it to get excited. Yes, you might watch them for planning tips or to see if you want to do a specific activity, but not to the extent that Disney fans do. This is another thing that makes Disney different from other trips.

A core memory for me as a child was when Disney sent their planning video on DVD for us to watch before our first trip. I remember how exciting it was to sit down as a family and get a teaser of what we were going to experience. Although we're long past the era of discs, I have watched the same video on YouTube many times since then.

I also love that there are certain things that Disney Adults get that other people just don't. There are secret jokes about Disney World and the films that, unless you're a devout fan, would go straight over your head. People who aren't a part of the fandom won't understand the hatred for Beverly, the urge to throw hair bobbles on Everest, or why Eddy Maserati is an absolute legend.

It gives us insight into the community and allows us to understand each other in ways that other people just won't. That is what being a part of something is all about, and it is something that should be celebrated, not hated.

The Disney fandom dates back a lot earlier than people would assume. The first Mickey Mouse Club launched way back in the 1920s. Many believe Disney launched this club when, in fact, it was a man named Harry Woodin. Walt only became involved when he received an invitation from Woodin to visit for a meeting. The group's intention was the same as any other recreational group for children: companionship, community, and encouraging good values.

As expected, the club was eventually used for economic gain. Mickey Mouse merchandise was distributed and only grew in popularity as the club grew in size. Walt had the theory that the more Mickey he could get into homes, the more it would encourage those to watch his films.

Disney is regularly criticised for its greed when it comes to commercialising its stories, but isn't it a love for its stories that creates the initial desire to experience them and own the merchandise? At the end of the day, none of this would've come to be if it wasn't for the simple fact that people like Mickey Mouse.

As mentioned in a previous chapter, Disneyana is a term used for the sale and procurement of Disney collectables. However, alongside that, there is also a Disneyana fan club. This is one of the oldest and largest fan clubs that has branched off from the original Mickey Mouse Club.

Similar to the D23 Fan Club, but separate from the Disney company, this club offers membership and events for Disney fans. Unlike the Mickey Mouse Club, which was aimed at young members, this club is for Disney fans of all ages who wish to join in 'preserving and sharing the rich legacy of Walt Disney.'

Disneyana has its own dedicated website and social media pages. It runs its convention and newsletters alongside other fan events. It even has a National Board of Directors where, as required by its law, a nominating committee is appointed every two years to assemble the new slate of directors. It all sounds very fancy and official, and I'm all for it. World domination, guys, it's happening.

Disney also hosts its own events, which are a great way to bring the community together. These are seasonal events at Magic Kingdom, like Mickey's Not-so-Scary Halloween Party nd Mickey's Very Merry Christmas Party. Also gaining more popularity over the years are after-hours events, where the park loses and is only open exclusively for the guests with these tickets. Although children are allowed to attend these events, since they run until later in the night, the atmosphere is more adult-centred. We're one step closer to kicking those kids out of Disney!

Disney also hosts runDisney events in their parks. These are marathons, half-marathons and shorter runs. Guests who sign up receive merch and a medal when they have completed it. These events are unique because not only are you running around Disney Parks with Disney characters present, but Disney Adults, being who they are, also get super into the event. You will see those who will do the run in costumes and specialised outfits.

I'm not sure there is anything in the world that would make me run a marathon. But if anything is ever to get me off my arse, you better believe it's going to be Disney.

There are so many testimonials online about how being involved in runDisney has changed people's fitness journeys. At the end of the day, if it's Disney that motivates you, then bloody brilliant! I also love that this is another great thing to come out of Disney; people come together not only to celebrate the company but also to motivate each other to get healthy. Be that as it may, yoga in front of Cinderella's Castle is probably a little more my thing.

Though Disney organises fantastic events throughout the parks, fan-organised events have garnered the most attention in the past few years. Dapper Day, Bats Day, Gay Day, and Rock-a-billy Day are all events organised by fans who participate in the parks.

Dapper Day, originating in Anaheim, began as a small get together. The occasion now draws over 25,000 participants. It celebrates 'stepping out in style' and dressing up in a safe place where it doesn't feel like everyone is staring. Guests come in their most sophisticated attire, inspired by vintage classics, chic, and even contemporary looks. There is no additional cost other than your park ticket, and attendees come together for an afternoon ride on the Mark Twain Riverboat and a ride on the carrousel after dark.

Dapper Days are held at Disneyland CA and Walt Disney World Orlando twice a year in Spring and Autumn. Other events are also held outside of the parks during different times of the year. But I can absolutely say that getting dressed up and frolicking on the riverboat is going straight on my bucket list.

Gay Days was started nearly 30 years ago by a group of friends who wore red to the parks. This was a statement that those who are a part of the LGBTQ+ community are able to stand out rather than hide away. The event has now exploded, escalating into a six-day event with hundreds of thousands of attendees.

All wearing red, the event celebrates the gay community amongst Disney Adults and their families. Though there is pushback from Christian communities in Florida, Disney refuses to intervene and prevent this event. Cast Members are instructed to treat the park day just like any other.

Once again, this is another event launched by the fans, and what a beautiful moment it must be for those involved to see how the community comes together. The photos of the sea of red in Magic Kingdom are so moving, and I hope this event only continues to grow in the years to come. Take that Ron DeSantis.

Though Dapper Day and Gay Day receive the most attention, Bat Day and Rock-a-billy Day are also popular fan-run events.

both embrace the subcultures of gothic and retro within the Disney community. Fans come to the events dressed in themed outfits and makeup to celebrate their shared love of something alongside Disney.

These events are a perfect example of how Disney brings people together. A gothic Disney event feels pretty niche, yet it draws people in large numbers. I didn't even know about the DisneyGoth community until I started researching for this book, which shows how successful the event is at pushing the subculture out into the public eye.

I mean, if you want to take this a step further and really immerse yourself in the Disney community, you could quite literally move to one. Disney Golden Oak is a resort-style living community near Walt Disney World. Hold the phone. Before you pack your bags, you should know that these luxury homes don't come cheap, with prices starting in the casual 2 million range. Fuck.

So, since I'm the kind of person who isn't sure if they can stretch the extra 20 dollars for Genie+, I have a feeling this is a little out of my price range.

As envious as I am of the residents of Golden Oak, it is so cool that this is even an option. Not only is this an option, but people are also fighting for this opportunity. So much so that in 2022, Disney announced the Storyliving by Disney community. Two new locations in North Carolina & California where Disney Adults can live out their Disney dream.

Now, this is the ultimate step for a Disney Adult, and if anyone wants to let me kip on their sofa there, then... please. You just know that these places are going to be a thing of beauty. Run by Cast Members and built by Imagineers, talk about quite literally living in a Disney story.

Anytime humans are brought together, it should be admired. The way that Disney Adults rally together for just about anything is such a beautiful thing. Don't get me wrong, I'm going to slam past you at rope drop, but a few hours later, I'll be doing the Mexican wave with you at Fantasmic like nothing ever happened.

There are many fandoms out there with loving communities, and I salute you guys. But Disney is different; it's on a whole other level. There are so many events created by fans and so many more activities. It feels like anything is welcome, and you can be whoever you want to be. Can you imagine if the outside world was more like that?

So keep supporting each other, as this is the part the haters hate the most. Disney creates a place where people can unapologetically be their authentic selves—a way of expression but also unity. So hold the hands of your Disney brothers and sisters, and just like the photo pass photographer does in Hollywood Studios, let's get the world's biggest group photo in front of the Chinese Theatre.

Lydia's Favourite Disney Scores

1. Nemo Egg (Main Title) – Finding Nemo.
2. This Land – The Lion King.
3. Stuff We Did – Up.
4. A Bug's Life Suite – A Bug's Life.
5. The Medallion Calls – Pirates of the Caribbean.
6. Bundle of Joy – Inside Out.
7. Transformation – Beauty & The Beast.
8. Waiting for the Lights – Tangled.
9. Vuelie – Frozen.
10. Define Dancing – Wall-E.

Step 9: Be the New Generation

One of the things I love most about Disney, and I suppose what's at the core of this book, is how multi-generational it is. Despite the argument of who it's for and everything Disney Adult, it has been true since the dawn of Disney that the company's work is to be enjoyed by those of all ages. Walt Disney said, "I do not make films primarily for children. I make them for the child in all of us, whether we be six or sixty."

Disney always had to appeal to the market of older consumers, since they were going to be the ones spending the money. Parents buy the park tickets, the cinema tickets, and the merchandise for children. Whether Walt Disney intended his work to garner such an adult cult following will always remain somewhat unclear, but he certainly knew it could go that way.

In an interview with journalist Pete Martin, Walt spoke about how more and more adults are becoming interested in his films. Martin commented on how almost as **many** adults compared to children were going to see the movie Swiss Family Robinson and believed the same applied to Disneyland attendance.

Walt was happy that adults were beginning to understand that the things he builds are to appeal to them too. When Snow White was released, many adults didn't feel they could go and see it without a child, as it was universally believed it wasn't intended for them. Thankfully, we Disney Adults have evolved since then, and this is no longer the case. Despite that, this shows even as early as 1960, Walt was aware of the love for Disney from adults.

Could Walt have predicted what the Disney Adult would grow into? Who knows? But I believe the man was clever enough to have. Whether he did or not, even in the company's infancy, it was considered that grown-ups would also enjoy Disney.

If we look at this from a business perspective, this was excellent news. This widened Disney's market to just about anyone, which has allowed the company to grow as big as it has and achieve its successes.

Now, if I look at this from a more naive, pixie dust, and magic wands point of view, this is great because it creates a community where age sees no bounds. All of a sudden, the things that limit us because of our age no longer exist. Children aren't too young, and adults aren't too old. Imagine a world where it doesn't matter how old you are, just how much fun you're having. Guess what? You don't have to imagine it. It's motherfucking Walt Disney World.

As much as I want to be all, 'age is a state of mind, not a number' kinda bullshit, we all know that's not true. I couldn't get drunk on tequila while I was in primary school, just in the same way I won't be able to cartwheel when I'm 70. Not that I can do a cartwheel now.

As much as I'll always wave the flag for equality, it would be foolish to neglect the fact that there is age disparity, whether we like it or not. So, when you find something like Disney that unites people of all ages for one singular thing, it creates something quite beautiful.

A few months ago, I was on a train from Gatwick when I

decided to full-blown eavesdrop on a conversation. I didn't intend to; I wanted to stare out the window and think about how depressed I was to be back in the UK. Instead, I heard the word Disney, and my ears instantly pricked up.

On the table in front of me, a young girl sat down with an elderly couple. They didn't know each other, but they soon got into a conversation about where they had just landed from. 'Disneyland Paris', the young girl shared, and the couple immediately lit up. 'Oh, we love Disney,' they said, and the girl was thrilled.

The older couple explained that they had begrudgingly taken their grandchildren to Walt Disney World, expecting not to enjoy it. However, the lady spoke of how she immediately welled up at the sight of the castle despite never being that big of a fan of the films.

They spoke, at length, about how they enjoyed it just as much as their middle-aged children and young grandchildren. They said there were things there for every age, and you don't need to be a Disney fan to be moved by the magic they create.

I didn't put my earphones back in for the whole journey; instead, I stayed fixated as an onlooker while the conversation unfolded in front of me. Because they were absolutely right, it can and should be enjoyed by all ages. Not only that, but this was another example of Disney uniting a group of total strangers on a random train on a Thursday afternoon. I genuinely believe that had that girl just got off a plane from Tenerife, the exchange wouldn't have been in-depth, and it certainly wouldn't have been as magical. Disney wins again, folks.

This book touches on how Disney has changed over the years and how it has branched out into films and TV shows with more adult themes. Even the Theme Parks are changing to suit adults, with alcohol and after-hours events.

Disney is constantly evolving to appeal to an older crowd. Take a ride on Smugglers Run, and you tell me that ride was made with children in mind? I was crumbling under the responsibility of my role as a pilot. I had the gunners behind me, people who I had never met before, screaming at the top of their lungs. I felt like I was in Gordon Ramsay's Hell's Kitchen. It took 10 minutes of blowing into a paper bag to calm me down afterwards. Tower of Terror was less stressful. Honestly, you will not be able to go on that ride and then look me in the eyes after and tell me Disney World is for kids.

A lot of conversations surrounding the origin of Disney Adults centre around whether one visited Disney World as a child. This is interesting, as it's undeniable that nostalgia plays a huge part in people's love for Disney. In my personal experience, growing up watching Disney and being fortunate enough to get to visit the parks is at the centre of why I love Disney.

Captain Jack Sparrow: 'We have our heading'

Peter Pan: 'Here we goooo'

Narrator: 'From the magic within our hearts, to the adventure beyond the horizon... there's only one Disney.'

If this struck a chord somewhere deep in your memory, then that means, like me, you were a part of the Disney VHS generation. For those born post-millennium, don't worry, I will explain. VHS was the dominant home video format in the pre-2000s and allowed people to watch films at home on tapes before DVDs were invented. If you don't know what a DVD is, then you probably aren't old enough to be reading this book, but I am not here to judge you.

Somewhere deep in my mum's loft, tangled between old photo albums and forgotten Christmas decorations, is our

Disney video collection. The Lion King, Aladdin, Tarzan, and all the films that I remember pushing into the video player and probably having to manually rewind because I hadn't bothered to last time. These instantly remind me of my childhood years.

Not everyone is able to recall their childhood fondly, but for most, they will look back on their younger years with fondness. Missing the years of innocence, naivety, and unbridled joy. This is why when we're reminded of something from our childhood and feel nostalgic, it brings a sense of safety.

The past is the only thing in our lives that is factually set; we're living in the present, and the future is uncertain, but we know absolutely that we have already had happy days. Recalling those brings us hope for more of that happiness in the future. A synonym for nostalgia is homesickness, which I think puts the whole thing into context.

There have been many scientific studies on nostalgia. One study found that listening to music we find nostalgic raises our temperature. It quite literally warms our hearts. Reminiscing on the past helps us give our lives meaning by reflecting on the positive experiences we've already had.

Is this the origin story of every Disney Adult? Absolutely not. For some, I believe it is a contributing factor but it's not a compulsory experience. It can go both ways. My brother grew up as a Disney kid, but he has no interest in it in adulthood. Whereas for me and my sister, it is basically our entire personality.

The best example I can give is that I grew up watching Wishes at Disney World, and although a lot of people will give me stick for this, I much prefer Happily Ever After. So, despite the fact that Wishes is the more nostalgic show for me, I welcomed the upgrade with open arms and now enjoy it far more.

One of the things I love most about Disney is that you can go from watching Cinderella, a film from the 50s, to watching a more modern film like Moana in the blink of an eye and not feel a disconnect despite them being decades apart. Cinderella is certainly nostalgic for me, but I loved Moana even when it was released during my adulthood. I enjoyed that film for the film itself, not because little Lydia loved it.

I have friends who didn't grow up on Disney and found it in their later years and still love it just as much as I do. Having Disney as a part of your childhood may be an additional factor in why you love it, but it doesn't define a Disney Adult.

Disney has cleverly played on nostalgia over the years. Take the remakes for example, they're wildly popular because there is already so much love for the originals. There is a part of us that cannot bring ourselves to neglect them. It also creates this beautiful parallel where adults who went to see the original in the cinema as children are now able to take children to see the remake. Some parents saw The Lion King in the cinema in 1994 and then took the next generation to see the remake in 2019. And so we're all connected by the great Circle of Life.

Pixar has also used this to its advantage over the years. We all grew up watching the original films when they were released in the 1990s/00s. Pixar then started to make sequels to these films many years later, but it transposed the narrative so that it was relatable to the Pixar children, who were now all grown up.

As children, we watched Andy play with his toys, and then, as we left school and started adulthood, we saw Andy emotionally give them away. Children also loved this story, but it hit our generation more deeply due to its relatability. The same thing happened with Monster's University: The prequel showed them as younger monsters experiencing college life, which is where a lot of the original viewers were at with their lives.

Although I don't see this theme continuing, I can't see Toy Story 5 having the plot line of Andy being denied a mortgage and dealing with the cost-of-living crisis. However, the concept has undoubtedly worked until now and has only strengthened the connection that we feel by growing up with these stories.

The way I felt as a child walking down Main Street, USA is no different from how I feel as an adult. Disney is the perfect way for us adults to explore our inner child and feel less like adults. I don't know who wouldn't want to go to a world where responsibility doesn't exist. As Walt himself said, 'Growing old is mandatory, but growing up is optional.'

It's a wonderful thing for a child to get to go and experience Disney, and someone who is 2, 3, or even 4 generations older than them could go and have an equally wonderful experience. I don't know how to emphasise how rare that is.

Everyone talks a lot about wanting to wait until their children are older to go to Disney. That way, they can remember it and get more out of it. I completely understand why people would make this choice, especially with the costs associated with it. However, if this is financially viable for you, then you shouldn't let this put you off.

No, your baby isn't going to remember being hugged by Mickey or playing in Fantasyland, but you will. And you shouldn't deny yourself that memory if it is something that you want. Many people say that one day, your children won't shout after the characters with as much joy as they do when they're younger. That you should enjoy it while it lasts. This is total bullshit, as I actually shout louder now, but I totally see where they're coming from.

Disney is profoundly magical for children, and as much as I joke about a fantasy multiverse where children don't exist in

Disney World—no, seriously, think about that for a moment. In reality, I would never want that to happen, as there is something so lovely about getting to see children experience the magic of Disney.

Walt wanted to create a place where children and adults could have fun together, but also have their own fun. At Disney Parks, there really is something for everyone, but there are also things that can be enjoyed by anyone. It doesn't matter how old you are; everyone finds Olaf funny. It doesn't matter how old you are; hugging Mickey will bring you so much warmth. It doesn't matter how old you are; the fireworks are going to have your mouth wide and your eyes wider. I genuinely didn't mean for that to sound as dirty as it did.

As children, we're eager to grow up to be adults, craving freedom without understanding responsibility. We role-play that we're working adult jobs and play with dolls like we're parents. Disney provides a space where suddenly none of that feels as important. Children can just be children.

Adult / Child psychiatrist Amanda J. Cahlhoun, MD explained why people have such an attachment to Disney even as adults. She commented on how Disney provides an escape for adults from real life. Adult life can be stressful, overwhelming, and sometimes just plain old boring. Disney is a magical alternative to this.

There are so many forum posts where people share their stories about feeling like Disney has healed the trauma they experienced as a child. Getting to explore their inner child in a safe place, something they never got to do as a minor, means a lot to them.

There are also many articles online quoting psychologists saying that trauma and mental health are at the root of Disney

Adults. Although I think it's so lovely that people are having positive mental and emotional experiences as a result of Disney, I don't think these articles could be more misleading.

It's essential to recognise the positive impact it has had on people who have been through difficult times. Still, it's also not fair to immediately associate everyone with this exact scenario. Mental health isn't the driving force behind Disney Adults, of course there is some relationship, but to claim that this is the only reason that people like Disney is just factually incorrect.

Growing up literally sucks. Being an adult fucking sucks. Why wouldn't I want to escape my problems in a magical fantasy world where I can live on sugar and spend my days on rides? If anything, it's those who wouldn't want to do that who I think need some kind of psychiatric help.

Own your position as a Disney Adult and be proud of this generation for having passion. Celebrate the new generation of children who are going to keep this fandom alive. So whether you're a Disney kid, Disney Adult or Disney pensioner, fucking enjoy it. Because if a trip to Disney gives me a couple of weeks to escape the rapidly impending need to 'adult', then I'll just take a one-way ticket please love.

Lydia's Favourite Disney Shorts

1. Once Upon a Studio – Walt Disney Studios.
2. Olaf Presents – Walt Disney Studios.
3. Geri's Game – Pixar.
4. Lava – Pixar.
5. Silly Symphonies Flowers and Trees – Walt Disney Productions.
6. Bao – Pixar.
7. Float – SparkShorts.
8. For the Birds – Pixar.
9. Cycles – Short Circuit.
10. Purl – SparkShorts.

Step 10: Stop Everything For D23

As mentioned previously, D23 is the official Disney Fan Club. And as much as I'm campaigning to make Disney Adults the unofficial but more legendary fan club, I can't go through this book without recognising D23. Because as a Disney Adult, you can't help but get involved.

D23, named after the year that the Disney company was founded, is most well known for its bi-annual D23 Expo. It was announced by Bob Iger in March 2009 and is similar to the setup of the famous San Diego Comic-Con. Initially, it started as an annual event, but the following year, it was changed to bi-annual, with Destination D happening in the years that the Expo did not.

I've never been fortunate enough to attend one of the D23 events, although I have my fingers crossed for the future. However, you can still livestream everything that's happening from all over the world. I watch it every year with bated breath, absolutely buzzing for whatever they're going to announce about Disney's future.

The Expo features things like panels discussing future projects, upcoming attractions, award ceremonies, pop-up stores, exclusive merch, celebrity appearances, fan contests, history presentations, memorabilia trading, and archival exhibits.

The eighth D23 Expo took place this year, and there have been many iconic moments over the years. Every event grows bigger and bigger, showing how the Disney fanbase only continues to grow. Taking place at the Anaheim Convention Centre in California, events are held in four areas: the D23 Area, Stage 23, Storytellers Theatre, and Walt Disney Studios Theatre.

Though the event has dramatically shifted in size since the first in September of 2009, the debut event will forever go down in Disney history. That year they announced a Fantasyland expansion, the 4th Pirates of the Caribbean film, and a new Muppets film.

A couple of years later, the 2011 Expo saw the return of the Disney Legends ceremony. The legends, chosen by a selection committee, honour talented individuals in the Disney company and recognise their contribution to its legacy. This ceremony began in 1987 and used to take place at Walt Disney Studios. However, it now takes place in front of an audience at the Expo.

I can say with unfaltering confidence that there has never been anything I have wanted more in life than to be a Disney Legend. But I hope for everyone's sake it never happens because I would be unbearable. Like seriously, I would have it tattooed on my forehead.

By 2013, attendance was estimated to be around 65,000. Visitors were given first looks at live-action films and animated films like Frozen. Lucasfilm made its first appearance. There were also exclusive looks at the upcoming Avatar land in Animal Kingdom and Shanghai Disneyland. For the first time, the D23 Expo in Japan happened in the same year.

2015 was an even more exciting year. If that could even be possible? An unbelievable number of incredible films got previews, like Finding Dory, Zootopia, Moana, and Coco. Captain America: Civil War footage and concept art for Doctor Strange were shown. This was also a massive moment for Star Wars fans, as Lucasfilm presented a first look at Star Wars: The Force Awakens.

Now, I don't consider myself to be much of a Star Wars fan; as a cinephile, I appreciate the franchise, but it just doesn't get me as much as others. However, I have seen so many videos of fans at D23 reacting to this first look, and every single time it gives me chills. There have even been times when there has been a bit of dust in the air while I've been watching them. I just love watching **people** get so hyped about something, even though it's not something I'm as personally passionate about. Imagine that, eh?

2017 & 2019 included very much of the same: first look at upcoming films, cast announcements and concept art for park expansions. You're starting to get the idea now. However, it did feel here that the original content somewhat declined, and the first looks were exclusively live-action and sequels. But we know that's what the Disney roster was looking like at this point. However, 20th Century Studios, now a part of the Disney family, joined the Expo in 2019 to share some of their upcoming work.

I think you know which year that will take us next. Unfortunately, due to the COVID-19 pandemic, the 2021 Expo was pushed to 2022, and we are now on even-numbered years. Because of this, I followed along with the 2022 Expo religiously. I feel like the withdrawals made me all the more excited about it.

The setup was the same as in previous years. However, there were some pretty exciting announcements for the Disney Parks.

Happily Ever After fans (me) rejoiced at the announcement of its return. And by rejoiced, I mean I screamed my fucking head off.

It was also exciting to hear about all the plans for the Disney100 celebration coming in the following year, which I very much took advantage of in the UK.

This section of the book is the very last one I'm writing, as I did my best to hold out for D23 2024. There is a lot to break down from this year, but also not much at all. The park announcements were massive, but the film announcements were very sparse.

Finally, everything we've been waiting to be confirmed, including the end of Dinoland and the Beyond Thunder Mountain Project, was officially announced. There were some expected additions like Villain's Land in Magic Kingdom as well as Indiana Jones & Zootopia coming to Animal Kingdom. Then there were some surprises, like the Monsters Inc. land at Hollywood Studios and Cars coming to Magic Kingdom. All of this is very exciting, and even though I may be retired by the time most of it opens, it means I'll have more free time to actually enjoy it.

The other parks weren't spared from the love. A new Lion King ride is coming to Disneyland Paris. We've got a new Coco ride and Marvel expansion at Disneyland California. The first ever Walt Disney animatronic, which I don't know about you, is going to bring out all of my feelings.

Hopefully, we can avoid delays and other drama that slows down these expansions, and then things will really pop off in the next few years for Disney Parks. There are a lot of original rides coming, and just in the nick of time, as Universal is just about to really step up their game in Orlando.

Speaking of originality, yep, you guessed it, we've got to talk about the film announcements. Now, don't get me wrong, when it comes to D23, I am glued to my phone, eagerly awaiting what they're going to announce. With every new reveal, I'm there trembling. New Snow White trailer? Tears. Stitch first look? Sweating. Incredibles 3 announced? Crying, screaming, throwing up.

The 'unoriginal' announcements, per se, are the ones that get our attention, as we know exactly what we're in for with those stories. It's safe, and even if it doesn't hit the mark, we're still going to enjoy the experience somewhat. I back that logic all the way.

However, out of all of the film announcements, and I'm focusing more on Walt Disney Studios & Pixar than Lucasfilm, etc. Only one original film was announced, and there were very few things we didn't already know about. Again, I get it, Frozen 3 was always going to get more cheers than Pixar's new film Hoppers that no one knows crap about.

After the high of the new trailers and new sequels wore off, I found myself in the middle of bottomless brunch (I'm not even kidding), zooming in on the D23 schedule, in disbelief that the panel was over and there wasn't more content to be announced.

We are going through the IP phase of storytelling, where everything is a remake, adaptation, or sequel. I know that they generate the most buzz, and I'm guilty of contributing to that. To give credit, this is the first D23 in a while that we haven't had a live-action remake announcement. But I wish Disney would take more risks and give more people the opportunity to create stories just as they did with animation and their SparkShorts and Short Circuit programmes.

Disney needs to invest more in experimental film-making.

The company made its way onto the map with its pioneering efforts, and it needs that incentive back. I think it is the best way for them to get the best new original film and TV. But hey, that's just one girl's opinion. That doesn't mean I don't want a live-action Hercules, though.

I love the time of year for the D23 Expo; even though I haven't attended, you can feel the buzz online from the Disney fandom. It is lovely to see on social media how the fans come together to celebrate the company that we all love so much.

One year, I was on holiday in Spain during the convention, and even then, it consumed our entire holiday. You can take the girl out of Orlando, but not Orlando out of the girl. Me and Beth were sharing a room, and I was literally standing shouting the announcements to her through the bathroom door.

Although children can attend and it is enjoyable for all ages, it is undeniable that this is aimed at the older fans. The queues for the panels can be as long as 5 hours to get a reservation, something that may be difficult for children to endure. Disney Adults, on the other hand, are more willing to suffer!

Fans camp out overnight to be the first in line to get their hands on the exclusive merchandise. Despite these more intense parts of the D23 Expo, there is still the Expo floor, where guests can wander around and experience the exhibits. There are also numerous photo ops that people can take advantage of.

Like many fan expos, Cosplaying is taken very seriously at D23. Disney cosplaying has always been a huge part of the fandom, just like many. Masses of attendees will go in costume, modelling some incredibly unique designs. People will take photos with each other and celebrate the effort that they have gone to. There is even a competition for those who want to enter.

They call the D23 Expo the ultimate Disney fan event, and that couldn't be more accurate. It is a crack den for all Disney Adults, and if you want a magical Disney day, this is exactly where you need to be. But also, as a nerd like me, I love the idea of immersing myself in not only the Disney world (punny) but also amongst the fantastic creatives who bring it to life. I'm such a fan girl over those people.

Although the Expo is the most significant part of D23, it isn't exclusively that which is the fan club. Destination D also makes up the events that happen the year the Expo isn't on; these vary in themes and structure. You can keep up to date with what's happening on the D23 website and social media. There is also a wealth of other unique D23 events that take place.

To access the events, you need to be a D23 member. You can sign up for free on their website and become a general member; here, you will receive limited access to events and the FanFare newsletter.

However, you can upgrade and pay for a Gold membership, which will get you a Gold membership card. This unlocks access to more events and offers. You also get the gold member collector set and an annual Disney Twenty-Three publication subscription.

This level of membership is not required if you want to try to get D23 Expo tickets; however, it will come with benefits such as shorter queues, priority seating, etc. To get these perks, you have to be a gold member when you buy the Expo tickets, as this will be stated on the ticket itself.

A wealth of content can be found on the D23 fan club, even as a general member. D23 has its own podcast called 'D23 Inside Disney', which is separate from Giovanna Fletcher's 'Journey to Magic' podcast. Both give you insights into the Disney company and the latest news to come from it.

There is also a D23 newsletter, news forum, recipes, videos, and quizzes. In summary, you have the perfect formula to make you procrastinate to fuck during the workday. Been there.

It also has information on Disney collections, such as Disney+, Pixar, Star Wars, Marvel, Disney Parks, Disney Princess, Disney fucking everything. You see where this is going.

And if you really want to dive deep and get a total bollocking from your boss, there are The Archives. This is a deep glowing hole of absolutely everything Walt Disney. So, if you want to give your eyes a break from the black-and-white of Wikipedia, which I really need to do more of, this is where you want to be.

Other fan events occur separately from D23. Marvel and Star Wars celebrate their own individual events. There is also Star Wars Day and Disney+ Day, where fans celebrate their fandoms. Disney uses the day to treat fans to news and content. The Disney Parks also get involved in the fun, hosting their own events.

Though there are many other unofficial fan clubs run by the fans themselves, it's nice to have an official source for information and the excitement of upcoming projects. I can't keep falling for Mouse Trap News. And nothing gets me more excited than watching D23 weekend live. I'm there with my Mickey Ears on, popcorn in my bucket, and absolutely loving everything that comes out.

I get second-hand excitement from the fans that get to go, and although it's so lovely to get the merch and all the news, the integral part of it all is the celebration of the Disney community. Thousands of fans come together with one common interest. It's the true place of worship for the Disney Adult, and one day I will make damn sure I'm there to soak it all in.

Lydia's Walt Disney World Hacks

1. Never buy water. You can get free ice water from all quick-service counters.
2. Use the shops on Main Street USA to skip through the crowds and get some air con.
3. Hold up glow sticks to find each other during the fireworks crowds.
4. Bring zip lock bags to put your valuables in on water rides, no paying for lockers.
5. Check Disney bus times on the app before heading to the bus stop, saves time waiting.
6. The Mickey Ears in the parks are better than online / at Disney Springs.
7. Take photos of your tickets in case you lose them.
8. Buy cheap lanyards before you go to put your tickets in, this makes them easier to scan, especially if you're using Lighting Lanes.
9. Independent Attraction companies, like FloridaTix, offer great deals on park tickets, especially during special sales like New Year's and Black Friday.
10. There is never enough time to do everything, remember to just enjoy the things you do get time to do.

Step 11: Be Ready to Fight the Haters

For this book, I've been to the far ends of the internet, including places I wasn't sure I was going to come back from.

Reddit. Let me tell you, that place is dark. It was like watching a child drop a Mickey Premium Bar straight out of the packet over and over until you question if you'll ever feel happiness again.

I didn't come out of there the same. I came out feeling dirty, like my Minnie ears had been steeped in thick tar, the bow never to be seen again. People really are hyper-fixated on shitting all over Disney Adults on there. I came out questioning whether I really was just a victim of consumerism. Am I totally lost in my privilege?

Then I was like, 'No Lydia, don't let the haters get to you'. So I got on a fresh pair of Minnie Ears, played You Are the Magic 3 times over while I had a cigarette and pulled myself together. Because this is the entire point of this book: not to let them get us down and ruin this for us. So let's crack the fuck on.

I don't condone violence. No, seriously, I don't want to see any of you throwing hands outside of It's a Small World. You know we aren't risking any lifetime bans around here. But a little heated debate never hurt anyone? And besides, we have a right to defend ourselves, don't we?

Whatever it is that riles people up about Disney Adults so much, we'll probably never know. However, adversity is a part of life. People are always going to hate on whatever you're doing, whether it's Disney, your relationship, your lifestyle, or the unholy amount of savvy b you can get down you on a Friday night in the pub. People are always going to have something to say.

Everyone is entitled to have their own opinions. Many people just don't like Disney for whatever reason; maybe they're not into films, animation, or theme parks. And that is absolutely okay. It's weird but okay. There are a lot of things that other people like that I don't, but I'm more than happy to let them crack on.

For example, I am a massive nerd and totally proud of it, but Lord of the Rings has just never got me. I don't know why and don't know what it is, but it just isn't my thing. However nothing about fans of the franchise bothers me one single bit.

This goes even further and out of film. I'm not a massive music fan, and I don't get excited about new releases. I'd much rather listen to the same Disney playlists and the bangers from Smooth Radio all day. So you'll never see me camping overnight for a Harry Styles concert or waiting until midnight for a new album release. But that is just me and my preferences. I admire those who go to these extreme lengths for the things that they love; it shows passion. I would do the same thing if it were Disney.

That leads us nicely to my next point. Going above and beyond for Disney. It's no secret that Disney fans are willing to go the extra mile for the company they love. They will stay up until 3 am in the UK to watch the live stream of the last-ever showing of Wishes. They will travel to London to see exhibitions and spend ll their money on trips (it is me, I am they). I can understand why some wouldn't get why people wanted to do that. If you don't like Disney, of course you're not going to spend your time and money on it, just like I wouldn't for Harry Styles. Sorry Harry, mate.

So why do people hate Disney fans going above and beyond for the thing they love more than other fan groups? I believe it comes down to just not understanding it. People find it hard to accept things they don't understand; you only have to look at history to get that. Wars have literally been started over people not liking things they can't understand.

We will never be able to comprehend everything in this world. You could be the most intelligent human on the planet, but you still won't because not everything can be explained by science and numbers. Fuck me, we're getting deep now. Strap in, lads. Life would be a lot easier if we could just accept what we don't understand, that people are entitled to enjoy different things.

As touched upon earlier, the hatred of Disney Adults has gone so far that even psychologists are expressing their opinions on it. Making claims like the reliance on Disney stems from trauma and emotional issues. It feels pretty crazy to me that people could place that opinion on such a large, diverse group of people who share one common factor.

There are a lot of us; the Disney Adult community is honestly huge. When you delve deep into social media, you will find hundreds of thousands of people who proudly display their love for Disney—and that's without the closeted ones. This is where these claims don't make sense to me. How is it that hundreds of thousands of people have all experienced the same trauma and are using the exact same coping mechanism? It feels like a bit of a shot in the dark.

Now, let's say this is correct. That all these people have been hurt and are using Disney to heal. What the fuck is wrong with that? I've seen much worse coping mechanisms. You should've seen teenage Lydia when she fell out with her parents. Also, who are these people to think they have a right to comment and assess people's mental state? I mean, how far is it going to go before people just go, 'Yeah, fairs, it's nice that you enjoy something.'

What if we switched it around and considered the psychology of those who are so quick to show resentment? Why would someone be so intent on ruining something for someone? My mum raised me to believe that they're just jealous, but it's possible this could run deeper into their psychology. What are they lacking? What happened to them? Do they have trauma? No idea. Because it's none of my fucking business.

Now, this has all gotten a little too serious for my liking. I can't help myself; I'm clearly psychologically unhinged. So let's dial it down a notch before we all start crying and calling our therapists. The main point here was not to take people who hate it too seriously. And despite my little lash-out, I do stand by that.

Rewind to a couple of years ago when I was in a new office. I work as a freelancer, so I find myself in new offices frequently, sometimes multiple times a year. This was a new workplace. Hence, they hadn't quite sussed yet that I'm a raging Disney Adult.

I overheard a conversation going on behind me. They were discussing how it's scary that adults want to dress up like cartoon characters. They commented on how you can like something without making it your personality and that Mickey ears give them the ick.

I sat there pretending to be deep in work, minding my own business, when in reality, I was transcribing the entire conversation into The Florida Four group chat (me and my girls who repeatedly go to Disney World—yes, there are four of us, and yes, we have given ourselves a team name). It was just as I started typing the words, 'Lydia, what do you think?' in Messenger that I realised they were now directly addressing me.

I tried to play it off at first, but anyone who knows me knows that I am the worst liar in the whole world. My smile immediately gave me away. They all let out a simultaneous 'ah' and started awkwardly fiddling with their pens. Then came the apologies, 'we didn't mean to offend you', 'we don't mean you, just the really crazy ones.' One even got out a photo of a friend at Disney, like they were trying to prove they weren't racist by saying they had a black friend.

I honestly wasn't offended. They were sharing an opinion, and just because it's not one I share doesn't mean I need to get irate about it. Like I said to them, it's nothing I haven't heard before. Life would be ever so dull if we all liked the same things.

Because I'm a film nerd, I love it when someone disagrees with me on an opinion about a film. Then we get to debate, and that makes the conversation far more interesting. I also may walk away having learned something.

There is a way to have a healthy difference of opinion. It is hard when you're being attacked for something you're passionate about, but at the same time, it doesn't give you the right to attack someone just because they're not. You can have an exchange where you share your opinions and still walk away as friends. This is precisely what I did in the office that day; I didn't think any differently of those people, and neither should

I.

You also have to be able to hear people out, which I love doing when we talk about Disney. Disney is not perfect; there are some serious flaws. It comes with its own question of business ethics and morality within the company, just like every other large corporation on the planet. I'm not saying that every decision they make in that company is the right one, just like every decision I make in my day-to-day life isn't the right one. Fucking hell, they're not. But that is just the way it goes in the corporate world, for better or for worse. At the end of the day, it's a company that has to make money, and that comes with a slate of very difficult decisions.

It is also problematic when it comes to crafting an art; not everyone will interpret it in the same way. Disney Adults argue amongst themselves over the best films, scenes, storylines, songs, etc. Some of the best Disney arguments I have are within my group of Disney friends.

As a Disney Adult, I am also more than capable of accepting that not all Disney films are perfect. There are some Disney films I literally cannot stand that I know for a fact others love. Some of the films that I swear by, people won't give the time of day. Again, that's perfectly ok.

Not to mention the fact that Disney has gotten it wrong a few times, and not just in recent times. Even the Disney classics that I would cut my left big toe, hell even my right big toe off to protect, are problematic. You've got plot holes all over the place. Like, come on, you're telling me not a single other female in the kingdom had the same size shoe as Cinderella? Even a size 3 or a size 8 women's shoe has problems getting flip-flops in Primark from time to time.

Now more than ever, Disney is feeling the heat from its

onsumers and deeply loyal fans. They're arguing over repeated emakes, constant sequels, and lack of original content. Not o mention how Disney going 'woke', just like anything going voke, has triggered many people.

And I get it, I really do. Some of Disney's casting in recent years has been somewhat controversial. The 2023 remake of The Little Mermaid is an excellent example of this. Disney had no business casting who they did in that movie, and it was always going to probe a reaction. There was absolutely no need for them cast someone so fucking fit to play Prince Eric. And I'm being deadly serious now because I was one more undone chest button away from having a stroke.

The Parks aren't exempt from scrutiny either. I can't tell you how many times I've heard, 'it sounds like my idea of hell' during a conversation. Again, I get it. This kind of holiday isn't for the faint-hearted. It's tiring, impacted by weather, and you cram so much in. I feel you; there is a downside to a Disney holiday. But I am not taking any more crap from the Brits about waiting in queues when so many of you waited 10 hours to see a bloody coffin. RIP Ma'am.

But seriously, Brits are the last people who have the right to get riled up about this; I've seen people run for a sunbed in the Costa Del Sol like it's the bloody Olympics. A relaxing holiday, ay? Just come to Disney, I've never had a problem getting a sunbed there.

Don't get me wrong, there are times when I'm in the queue for Flight of Passage where I think how I would love to Holly & Phil this shit. But this is just another part of the Disney experience, and if you're not up for it, that's completely fine. Pussy.

Disney also does a lot to try to make the time in the queues pass quickly, with interactive aspects and entertainment. Not to mention the fact I spend the whole time trying to beat Beth in finding hidden Mickeys. They also use techniques such as preshows and holding areas to create the illusion that the queue is over.

I've also recently seen a lot of stuff on TikTok about how taking your children to Disney isn't exposing them to the right things—that they should be out in the world, embracing nature and having formative educational experiences. I agree entirely and encourage parents to take their children out into the forest or a woodland. Then leave them there, and you parents can head to Disney and have a much cheaper day out.

At the end of the day, no matter what your opinion on anything Disney is, all I can say is that if you can see little black girls watching The Little Mermaid trailer and not be moved by their excitement to be represented, then you're lacking some serious empathy. If you don't think children running up to their favourite characters in the parks, beaming with joy, isn't a significant core memory and joy in their childhood, then I say sod off and enjoy your stupid hike then. There is a reason that Disney World is the no.1 choice for Make a Wish Children, and it's not because it's educational.

Now, we've got to circle back to those Reddit threads. As much as I'm trying to pretend they don't exist. On the whole people are very defensive of Disney Adults, reminding us that when people are so negative about something so positive, it is normally because they lack what you have. And that isn't something to be happy about. If someone is genuinely so sad that they feel the only way to cope is to make other people unhappy, then the only way I can react to that is with sympathy.

At the same time, I can't pretend that sometimes the Disney haters have a point. As with everything in life, there is always someone who has to take things too far. And don't get me wrong, it's wildly entertaining for us onlookers, especially when people get naked on It's a Small World. To be fair, I'm in support of making that a permanent addition. Imagine how more bearable it would be with strippers on there.

Also, don't drink the fucking Splash Mountain water. I mean, there's no surprise we just had a devastating global pandemic when there are people out there consuming ride water. You detty, detty pig. And don't even get me started on the 'faith, trust and bitch dust' car stickers...

I believe at the centre of it all, and why we have all been titled 'Disney Adults' instead of just Disney fans, is that people still think Disney is only for children. Yes, as we've spoken about in previous chapters, that was the initial intended market. Of course, a lot of the content is family-friendly and to be enjoyed by all. Even if that was the case and the content wasn't at all intended for adults, I still don't think there is anything wrong with enjoying that.

Sometimes, we all get a little bit too lost in the concept of being an adult. Other than the law telling us that we're adults at 18, adulthood doesn't exist. Yes, there comes a time when you have to be independent and have a level of responsibility we never had to consider as a child. But isn't being an adult just a social construct, where the world tells you that you need to have a mortgage and start thinking about your pension at 20 years old?

In reality, none of us know how to adult because there isn't a way to do so. Given the choice, we'd all much rather not worry about any bills other than our Disney+ subscription. So if we want to tap into that inner child just for a moment, to escape the stresses and pressures that the world lumps into this adult title, why the fuck shouldn't we? Since when was there even need to **grow** up?

Again, Disney isn't just for kids, but there is a child-like wonder that comes with loving Disney. A parallel world where life is just as simple as wishing on stars and falling in love at a ball. With some wicked stepmothers and a sprinkling of dead parents thrown in there, but you get the idea.

This is part of the reason the internet wanted to deem us Disney Adults, to divide us from the children who also love Disney. And I'm not going to lie; I am accepting of that. Because there is a distinct difference between child Disney fans and adult Disney fans, adults pay for that shit themselves.

When all is said and done, we're never going to stop people calling Disney Adults cringe, whether we throw psychology at them, kill them with kindness, or just let them crack on. But I saw something on Twitter recently from author Ashley C. Ford that really soothed my Reddit sores. He said that when we talk about cringe, we're usually talking about how other people feel. We spend way too much time concerned with how other people think and way too little about how we think.

When it comes down to it, if you love Disney, what the fucking fuck does it matter if someone disagrees?

Lydia's Favourite Disney Adult Reddit Thread comments

1. like cmon guys the whole point in Disney is to come together with love. why tf u hatin bro moana was pretty good
2. Some people care too much about peoples innocent interests. Just say you're boring
3. People who hate Disney Adults are worse than actual Disney Adults
4. A lot of people on here get really irritated with how other people spend their free time.
5. "Get off social media" – my therapist.
6. Why would you feel the urge to defend disney adults? Who even thinks about them?
7. I like it because it forces my kids to spend time with us without complaining they'd rather do something else.
8. This is actually maddening because most of these stupid fucks are just there to resell the stupid bucket to even stupider fucks on ebay who want to pay 200 dollars to eat popcorn out of a dragons asshole apparently...
9. It's just a hobby. Most of us could use a few more.
10. Who the fuck are these people?

Step 12: Understand Why Disney is Different

Ok, on the whole, the last chapter was deep-fried defensive with a side of depression. I'm all for fighting for the cause, but think we need a bit of an uplift after that. So, let's break down the real reason we're Disney Adults. And in the grand scheme of things, it's not because of privilege, immaturity, or mental illness. I'm not saying I'm not mentally ill, but that's got fuck all to do with Disney.

The truth is we love Disney because it is different. There is so much that makes it unique. In this chapter, I'm going to go through all the things that I think set Disney aside from its competitors and what's contributed to my falling for it. If you don't already love Disney, you're going to after this chapter.

Disney is renowned for its attention to detail. Their films are full of easter eggs and subtle nods to everything that is Disney. Disney Adults love to pick these apart, and it's become a massive part of the fun to try to find all that is hidden within a Disney film. As a film-lover, one of my favourite parts of enjoying a story is breaking down all the hidden details. All of this contributes to the world the writer has created, and I just fucking love it.

There are more apparent details in Disney films, like characters showing **up** in different films—Rapunzel and Flynn Rider attending Elsa's coronation, Mulan's poster in Lilo & Stitch, or Mrs Potts and Chip being at Jane's camp in Tarzan. Then, some really hidden details that may, at first, go completely unnoticed. Bring on the examples...

Mulan is told, 'a girl can bring her family great honour in one way, by striking a good match...' (I know you sang those lyrics) In one scene, Mulan takes down the Huns by striking a match to light the weapon. Mother Gothel kisses Rapunzel's hair when she tells her she loves her most, the true source of her desire. Even Tamatoa has Aladdin's lamp in his treasure trove.

It's not uncommon to see elements of other Disney films show up. However, Pixar takes this to the next level by telling the future. No, it's not The Simpson's style of future telling, but they do make nods to upcoming Pixar films. Nemo can be seen in 3 different scenes of Monsters Inc, Doc Hudson is parked up in The Incredibles' Metroville, and a car version of the DunBroch family is seen hanging on a wall in Cars 2. This tradition isn't always consistent, but fans love to pick them out when they're there.

Specific details have become familiar to Pixar fans over the years. A113 will always be found somewhere deep within a Pixar film. This is a nod to the classroom number that most of the animators occupied at the California Institute of the Arts.

The Luxo ball and lamp regularly make appearances throughout the films; these icons are pretty hard to miss. Other than the lamp being the logo, these are both from Pixar's first short, Luxo, Jr. The much-loved Pizza Planet from Toy Story also shows up from time to time in the films, sometimes as just a van or a pizza box. It seems to have become Domino's for the Pixar world.

It should come as no surprise that this same attention to retail is used all around the parks. Disney is more than just an amusement park; its rides aren't limited to carousels or waltzers. Their attractions tell a story. From the minute you walk into the queue, you become a part of the narrative. The theming, the music, and sometimes even the smells all contribute to creating an atmosphere, a feeling, that the Disney imagineers aimed to create.

Classic fairground rides are used within the parks but with their own Disney spin. Splash Mountain is like a log flume ride, The Haunted Mansion is like a ghost train, and Thunder Mountain is a runaway mine train. What makes them different is the experience.

An example of this is The Haunted Mansion. It's above cheap scares and screams and instead details the story of the jealous Madame Leota and how she killed Master Gracey's fiancé so she could take him for herself. Distraught over his beloved's death, Master Gracey hangs himself, leaving Madame Leota to haunt the castle after her own death from old age. The storyline isn't always explicitly clear, but half the fun is unpacking it along the way.

The story is wider than the ride itself. The outside queue of The Haunted Mansion takes you through the gardens of the manor filled with gravestones and tombs, including interactive aspects to get you involved. There is even an engagement ring embedded into the concrete near the entrance, supposedly belonging to the Master's late fiancé (see if you can find it). You become a part of the story way before you take a seat on a doom buggy.

Those who are new to Disney may be confused as to why some of its more dated rides remain in the park, despite major refurbishments. There are many attractions in the Disney Park that were opening-day attractions and still remain functioning. Jungle Cruise is one of these, and it has become such a fan favourite that should Disney ever try to remove it, there is likely to be an uproar.

Some of these older attractions have become so popular that they have even been recreated at newer parks. For example, Pirates of the Caribbean has been modernised for Shanghai Disneyland. Yet, it still maintains that original feeling.

Imagineers leave no stone unturned during the creative process of designing and building a Disney attraction. John Hench, a Creative Director, commented on the similarities between film-making and theme park design. Many techniques are used to add depth and bring areas of the parks and attractions to life.

One way this is done is by forced perspective, a method used throughout Walt Disney World and other Disney Parks. The most well-known is Cinderella's Castle. The elements of the castle at higher elevations are reduced in size, like the stones and windows, to make the castle appear taller than it actually is. This is also used significantly in Pandora in Animal Kingdom with the floating mountains.

If you want to talk about attention to detail in Walt Disney World, then look no further than the centre of Animal Kingdom to the Tree of Life. The tree features 325 hand carvings of animal species; it is stunning from every angle. Detail is a huge part of Disney Imagineering; there is so much to it that it may go unnoticed at first glance.

Every manhole cover features the symbol of Mickey Mouse. Peanuts are found littering the pavement of Storybook Circus. Pascal hides among Rapunzel's gardens. Sunset Boulevard uses the original Starbucks logo. A key is left under the mat t Muppet*Vision 3-D. The paw prints of Lady and the Tramp re outside Tony's Town Square Restaurant. Cinderella has er own horse on Prince Charming Regal Carrousel (it has a old ribbon on its tail). A morse-code version of Walt Disney's pening day speech at Disneyland can be heard as you climb he stairs of the Main Street Railroad Station. And the list goes n and on (literally).

Imagineers take theming very seriously, from the lack of oilets in Liberty Square (as there were no toilets during that ime period) to the raised sidewalks of Frontierland. They ven pump smells into specific areas. For example, guests can mell bakeries throughout Main Street USA, which brings the onfectioneries alive and entices them.

Hidden Mickeys are another detail at the Disney Parks that love. A hidden Mickey is where Imagineers subtly represent Mickey Mouse, either in an attraction, or just around the park. These are a kind of Easter Egg hunt for the guests, something hat my friends and I have taken very seriously during our visits.

While at the park, if you ever hear random celebrating and cheering in the distance, either someone has just proposed, or a hidden Mickey has been discovered. This is just another impressive way Disney has included detail in its parks. Approximately 1,000 hidden Mickeys have been recorded, but since no official number has been released by Disney, who's to say there aren't even more?

We know all too well how protective Disney fans get about much-loved rides getting replaced. But Disney loves to pay homage to defunct rides. After the replacement of Mr Toad's Wild Ride devastated fans, Disney decided to leave a little tribute to Mr Toad in the pet cemetery outside of The Haunted Mansion. Mr Toad can also be found in The Many Adventures of Winnie the Pooh, the attraction that replaced it. Look for a picture in Owl's house of him signing over the deed of Toad Hall to Owl

Disney has done this many times before to pay tribute to the rides that once occupied the area. When Star Tours at Hollywood Studios was updated, the once-loved Captain Rex was replaced by the more recognisable C-3PO. However, luckily for Rex, he wasn't completely disregarded, as he can still be found in the queue for the attraction with a defective sticker on

A carved tribute of the old submarines of 20,000 Leagues Under the Sea: Submarine Voyage can be seen during the queue for Under the Sea – Journey of the Little Mermaid, the attraction that replaced it almost two decades later. Fuck me; those ride names boosted my word count. There are so many more of these tributes hidden among the Walt Disney World parks. Keep your eyes peeled, and you might just get a peek into the history of Walt Disney World. Now, that's a History lesson I would pay attention to.

Imagineers like to ensure authenticity when it comes to the parks. When it came to planning the Animal Kingdom park and the areas that are based on continents around the world like Africa and Asia, Disney wanted to get it right. To ensure the places were accurately represented, Imagineers travelled to those countries to research the culture and study the landscapes and wildlife.

When designing the popular Expedition Everest ride, Imagineers spent a grand total of six years creating it. During that time, they took many trips to the Himalayas to undertake research. Although the mountain is not a model of Mount Everest but a fictional mountain, it only adds depth to the story that the Imagineers have created.

Another part that I adore about visiting a Disney Park is what I ke to call the 'Disney Bubble'. The world is a scary place; even day-to-day life is filled with anxieties. Bills, taxes, politics, current affairs, eating your 5-a-day, spiders, knowing you should stop smoking but don't want to, cozzie livs. Life can quite quickly feel overwhelming.

When I visit Disney, I feel like I enter a bubble where nothing from the outside world can harm me. Walt Disney World is deep in Florida, very separate from the normal functioning, stressful AF world. But as soon as you drive under those gates, it feels like you're protected.

You're immersed in this magical world for the time you're there, and your daily concerns don't feel so detrimental anymore. Of course, I know as soon as I get back on the plane that life is going to slap me straight across the face again. But who doesn't want that little sabbatical?

Disney allows you to submerge yourself in the Disney stories that you love. You're no longer a spectator, like watching a sports game or a concert. Instead, you're right in the middle of the action. There are very few things out there that grant that opportunity to its fans. There aren't even many other films that provide that. Twilight fans can't go and get bitten by vampires, and Saltburn fans can't... Well, you get the idea. The ability to have this unique experience is another reason Disney is set apart from other fandoms.

When my alarm goes off for work in the morning, I respond with grunts and groans because, just like everyone else in the world, who can be arsed? But when my alarm goes off at 5am in Disney to get that virtual queue boarding pass and be at the front of the line for rope drop, I am absolutely bounding out of bed. There is nothing else in the world that turns people into such enthusiastic early risers.

Some people choose to plan their Disney holiday, and other prefer to wing it. Either way is completely fine. However, if you are a planner, then you know that there is an art to planning a Disney holiday. Those who, like me, have colour-coded planners and folders really do enjoy doing all the planning When I've been on other trips like backpacking, I have been super organised and have notes and pages of plans. But it isn't the same as planning a Disney trip, and that in itself makes it so unique.

It goes even further than this. Of course, the attention to detail is fantastic, as well as the ever-expanding parks that a lot of time, effort, and money go into. Yet, there are parts of Disney that run deeper than that. Disney does everything that it can to make trips as inclusive as it can, with child swap so adults can enjoy all the adult rides and baby care areas for breastfeeding mums.

The Disney Accessibility Service means that Disney can be enjoyed by everyone, no matter their requirements. Those who are unable to queue can apply for a pass to bypass the lines. You can get a return time so you can come back and skip the queue, then enjoy the attraction just like everyone else. Guests in wheelchairs can be accommodated at the front of the rides by trained Cast Members. Those with invisible disabilities will be treated with just as much care and respect.

I know there has been some controversy recently regarding some of Disney's changes to the DAS pass. My heart goes out to everyone who feels that this has impacted their experience at a Disney Park. I understand why Disney has to make these changes, but at the same time, I hope they continue to work on it so that it doesn't negatively impact anyone it was originally created to help.

All Disney shows, transportation, and resorts are accessible or wheelchairs and guests with additional needs. Disney also offers break areas and companion bathrooms that can be really helpful for Disney guests with cognitive disabilities.

Cast Members are trained to know that children and adults with disabilities do need to be treated differently than other guests. That they require more care and attention and that simply neglecting to acknowledge someone has a disability is ignorant.

Many Cast Members will understand sign language or have experience interacting with those with additional needs. This kind of service is rare, and I can't imagine how much it must mean to the person and their loved ones. Breaking down these barriers allows individuals to experience Disney just like any other guest would.

Disney Parks also takes their first aid very seriously. Stations are dotted all around the parks, and cast members are trained to know precisely what to do in an emergency scenario. If you're going to sustain an injury anywhere, Disney is a relatively safe place to do so.

Doctors can visit the resorts, and all staff will go above and beyond to ensure you're safe and cared for. They will even follow up with you after a said incident. I can't imagine how reassuring this must be if a guest is visiting with underlying health conditions. Be assured that Disney will be there to support you.

As mentioned in the previous Cast Member chapter, Disney takes hiring and training very seriously. The Cast Members play a huge role in making Disney different from other companies. Their amazing customer service stems from what Disney calls the 'Quality Service Compass'. These four points guide the employees in offering the best customer service they can.

Guestology, quality standards, delivery systems, and integration are all the points of the compass that Cast Members use to create the optimum overall experience. These may sound like words in an employee handbook, but when you break them down, they're actually very reassuring.

Compass point 2, for example, is the quality standards. This is separated into four sections: safety, courtesy, show and efficiency. These are in order of importance so employees know which to prioritise. Applying this to a working situation means that safety would come before show. If a Cast Member was about to perform but saw a child in distress, the child would be prioritised because it would fall under safety. Although Disney is committed to the performance, it is comforting to know that their guests are still the priority.

This all sounds very bureaucratic and as though HR has vommed all over it. But just like the pyramid of Imagineering, having guidelines to follow ensures quality control throughout. It is the key to successful management and, as a result, a successful business. And hey, it clearly works. So vom away HR.

Disney also places a heavy reliance on sound for its Cast Members. At Hong Kong Disneyland, they use a system called 'CostuMagic' where the Tinkerbell jingle plays when a Cast Member has completed their checks. This signals that they are ready as the character and can begin greeting guests. The Cast Members now recognise this sound as one associated with completion and becoming the character. I need to get that shit on my phone and use it in the morning.

There are so many ways that Disney has gone the extra mile to improve the guest experience. Ever wonder why Disney road igns are purple and red? Disney conducted an experiment by showing people flags of different colours. It turned out that the flags that were most remembered were the ones in that colour, hence the road signs.

Throughout Disney Parks, there are many secret rituals that people may only learn about once they encounter them—for example, opening Blizzard Beach by being the first to go down Summit Plummet, throwing the first pitch at Casey's Corner, or becoming a Galactic Hero at Space Ranger Spin. The Disney Parks are made up of so many potential core memories.

People are so quick to jump on Disney for everything they do wrong, yet I very rarely see people celebrating the good that they do. Disney makes huge charitable donations every year, as well as social investments and contributions to conservation. We all know about Disney's work with the Make-a-Wish Foundation. In the past 40 years, they have granted the wishes of over 150,000 children.

This goes beyond making children's Disney wishes come true. They also work closely with children's hospitals to organise events and experiences while children are receiving treatment. From Disney hospital gowns to in-theatre movies made available to children who can't make it to the cinema. There is so much more that they do. I could write a book on that alone.

I know I sound like a PR representative for the company, but I find it frustrating when people are so quick to focus on the bad and put on their blacked-out goggles when it comes to the good. The reality is that if Disney ceased to exist, it would do so much more harm than good.

Disney is doing a lot right now to promote diversity and ensure that everyone is represented in its media. However,

things have now gone the other way. Many are claiming they'r
forcing 'wokeness' into their stories, creating an environmen
where they can't do anything right.

Whatever your stance on Disney's choices, it cannot be denie
that they have long promoted diversity within their storie:
Back in 1992, Jasmine became the first non-white Disne
princess, and she was lovingly embraced. Since then, we hav
had princesses from all different lifestyles and background:
This allowed me, as a little girl, to learn about other culture:
and celebrate them.

However, inclusivity just wasn't represented the same wa
off the screen. Many of the diverse Disney princesses wer
actually voiced by white actresses. Disney is now creating
more opportunities for people from different backgrounds anc
accurately representing these cultures.

The narratives in older Disney films indeed fit particulal
gender roles; the princess has to be saved by the prince, anc
he is her happily ever after. Disney has dramatically shiftec
these stories in more recent years, and we now get to watch
princesses who desire more than just romance. Princesses are
just as strong and capable of saving themselves as being saved
It has been refreshing to experience these new stories. Although
it's nice to have modern love stories like Elemental, it is still so
important for little girls to grow up with independent female
role models.

When it comes to Disney, we know that anyone can be a
hero. I believe all of us have a lot of work to do to increase
representation and acceptance throughout society. I am proud
of Disney for all that they have done and continue to do.

One of the most regularly appearing criticisms of Disney
Adults is that we're being sucked into a corporate scheme, that

Disney is engineering a space to manipulate us into spending our money. I am not denying this for a second. But isn't this the point of a thriving business? Aren't Disney just very good at what they do? I don't see why, in the grand scheme of things, this is so evil.

Anything we experience that motivates or inspires us is likely to have been put out into the world with the intention of generating profit. When I watch films like Mulan and come away feeling inspired by that story, I know that it was created to make money. But that doesn't diminish the fact that it had a positive impact on me.

Disney has constructed a very clever business model, and hats off to them. But for me, at the core of it all, they're just really fucking good storytellers. And there is nothing I love more than a good story. Disney knows precisely how to make you feel. You can be having the shittiest of days, and you just need a good laugh with Olaf, or sometimes you just want to cry over an imaginary part cat, part elephant, part dolphin.

Visiting Disney is rarely just a one-and-done thing, especially for Disney Adults. I've just been on my 6th 'once in a lifetime' trip. Every Disney Adult has what I like to call their Disney crack addict moment. The point where you realise this isn't going to be something you do casually; it's going to be a full-blown, all-consuming addiction. This isn't a one-night stand or a situationship, you're going to stalk the fuck out of Disney until you know that it loves you too.

You'll probably be surprised to hear that my Disney crack addict moment wasn't perving over a cartoon villain or anything like that. It was actually the first time I met Belle as a child. I was ten years old and super self-conscious about going to the park in costume, convinced I was too old to be wearing a princess dress. Which is bullshit, by the way. Then, the minute I met her, she gave me that little bit of extra attention as we were wearing the same outfit, and nothing mattered to me any more.

When I walked out of that meet-and-greet, every insecurity I had disappeared entirely, and I skipped to the parade, happy that my dress was swishing at my ankles.

That moment is how I know that Disney magic exists. Even when I was selected to meet her again in my twenties, after I went to Enchanted Tales with Belle in a Beauty & The Beast top, it still felt just as magical.

Listen, guys, I know that is someone in a costume. I know they're paid to act like the character and be super nice to me. But when you're there, that isn't at all what you're thinking about. And why should it? So call the psychologists, because all I want is some of that Disney crack.

Disney is different for so many reasons. Their films are different, their parks are different. Just Google the Disney hug rule, and it will give you goosebumps. Whether it's for you or not, well, that's a personal preference. But for me, it's absolutely everything. Because I'm a mother-fucking Disney Adult.

Lydia's Favourite Walt Disney Studios Films

1. The Lion King (1994)
2. Beauty and the Beast (1991)
3. Moana (2016)
4. Tarzan (1999)
5. The Little Mermaid (2023)
6. Mulan (1998)
7. Zootopia (2016)
8. Encanto (2021)
9. Lilo & Stitch (2002)
10. The Princess and the Frog (2009)

Step 13: Own the Disney Adult Status

So here we are, the final step. This step isn't necessarily what makes you a Disney Adult, but instead, what I want to impart to you as we reach the end of this book.

I, myself, have had wobbles when it comes to being a Disney Adult. Hey, dark Reddit nearly ruined me. It's completely understandable to be concerned about what people think of you; we live in a society that fosters that attitude. I can scream in your face as many times as I can that it doesn't matter what they think (and it doesn't), but that's not going to change the fact that you're going to think about it.

Despite all that, if there is anything I want anyone to take from this book – other than the fact that I fancy a lion – it's that the most important person you'll ever make proud, is yourself. I can't tell you how much that will set you free when you make this a priority.

But Lydia, why is being a Disney Adult something to be proud of? Having a passion, something that warms up your insides and gives you goosebumps, is one of life's most incredible pleasures. Other than watching Mr Hauer-King's chest in The Little Mermaid.

I consider myself very lucky to have found something that brings me so much joy and makes me so excited. I genuinely sympathise with those who are yet to find something like that because, honestly, it's one of the best feelings in the world.

Believing in the magic of Disney isn't any different than putting your faith in horoscopes. Collecting Mickey Ears and Loungeflys is only like keeping up with the newest handbags and fashion. And what's so scary about Fairy Godmothers and wishing on stars anyway?

When I see Disney Adults supporting each other online, or how excited people get when Disney Parks UK runs a competition, it makes me so happy to be a part of such a kind community. Everyone is so eager to encourage and congratulate each other that status really doesn't matter. I will never understand why people get so irate about that. As Ricky Gervais so brilliantly put it, 'Just because you're offended, doesn't mean that you're right.'

I love that no matter what comes at me in life, no matter how tough it gets, I always have something like Disney to fall back on. I have a truly wonderful support system and so much in my life to be grateful for, but I'm also very lucky to have something else that I care for that much and can bring a little bit more of that sparkly sparkle.

When 17-year-old Lydia saved up her chip shop wages for 2 years to be able to pay for her Disney Park tickets, I wasn't concerned that I'd spent all that time and money on something so expensive. Instead, I was so proud of myself for working towards something that was going to bring me such euphoria.

Not everyone in life wants to save for mortgages or fancy cars. Who decided that's what we have to do anyway? We're all chasing a life on Instagram that doesn't even exist. I say that if it isn't truly what you want, then screw the glossy white kitchens, designer sandals, and expensive skincare and spend your money on something that is guaranteed to make you happy.

It couldn't be truer that if you sack off the expensive coffees for your entire life and save the money, you'd still never have enough money to buy a house anyway. Disney may be expensive, but at least it's more affordable than a house deposit! We really do only have one life; please don't spend it doing anything other than what makes you happiest.

I am constantly asked why it is I keep going back to Disney. And I can throw as many theories of happiness at you as I can, but when it comes down to it, the reason I keep going back to Disney is because I goddamn want to.

I'll never really be able to articulate how being at Disney makes me feel. It's a kind of happiness that, honestly, at one point in my life, I wasn't sure I'd ever be able to feel again. I have a lot of things in my life now that make me very happy, and most of them are a lot cheaper than a trip to Orlando. But I will always be chasing that Disney feeling.

I think Emma Watson's quote about Harry Potter couldn't be more applicable here: 'When things get really dark and times are really hard, stories give us places we can go, where we can rest, feel held.'

Why wouldn't I want to run to Belle like I'm 10 years old again? Get emotional when Tinkerbell flies across the night sky, or get so drunk in the Italy pavilion that the Eiffel Tower starts looking like it does on Soarin?

Just like the trend on TikTok, when I'm older and people ask me about my twenties, I can't wait to tell them how I was a fan girl. How I spent my time and money doing things that I loved, how I danced around the parks with my friends, laughing and making core memories. I wouldn't have changed this time for the world.

We're so quick to talk about romantic love, our first loves and the loves of our lives. But how about falling in love with life? How about the moments you knew that the bad times were worth it? I just have to clap eyes on that castle and something inside me tells me that everything is going to be ok, that I'm here for this reason, to feel this happy.

I would never encourage anyone to financially cripple themselves for a trip to Disney World or give the impression that the trip is going to solve all of their problems. Although it may solve a few. But if you are heading there, then know that you are about to create memories that will last a lifetime. It's a place that is constantly evolving but still maintains that same opening-day feel. You will both laugh and cry in a way you never have before.

So, of course, I'm going back! And yes, as people always say, there are other places in the world to visit, and I have been lucky enough to travel a bit outside of Florida. But I've also travelled around the world in one day, and I did it with a Blood Orange Margarita in my hand.

A family member once asked me, 'Are you ever going to grow up?' To this, I say, 'What is the actual meaning of that?'. The only part of growing up that matters is realising how good EPCOT is. So grow the fuck back down again, grab your Mickey ears, tell the pilot to head to the second star on the right, and fly your ass to the Disney bubble. Say it loud, and say it proud, 'Growing old is mandatory, growing up is optional.'

If you're heading on a Disney holiday soon, I wish you the best time. If you're escaping through a film, enjoy every moment. If you're immersing yourself in the Disney community, revel in it. And remember, you owe no one an explanation because you're a fucking Disney Adult, and you're proud.

So why has this weirdo made you buy her book? Well, for starters, she isn't a weirdo—not for loving Disney anyway. Over the past couple of years, I've torn myself up over whether I should release this book and what people might think both in my personal and professional life. Above all, I was concerned that dark Reddit was going to come for me with pitchforks screaming, 'Kill the beast!'

Then, I thought that the internal battle I was having was precisely the one I was trying to eradicate. I know the media have escalated the situation, and without their news articles, Disney Adults probably wouldn't have become such a phenomenon. But I wanted you guys to buy this book not only because I need the money for my Disney crack, but because I don't want anyone to feel ashamed about who they are.

Yes, when you put it into the perspective of what is going on in the world, people giving Disney Adults stick isn't the worst thing. The human world, it's a mess.

Trust me, if I could solve the world's problems and bring about world peace by writing some shits and fucks in a book, I would've been all over that many Disney Eras ago.

What I do know a lot about is Disney, and if me chatting shit about Disney bounding and sexy Disney Princes brings a little more light into the world, then bring it the fuck on dark Reddit.

Walt, I can't thank you enough for what you've brought to the world. Disney, thank you for always keeping the magic alive. To all my Disney Adults out there, thank you for being your beautiful selves. No matter what anyone ever says to you, remember who you are.

Acknowledgements

Since I was a little girl, I have fantasised about writing a book. As nice as fame and a potential closeted cocaine habit sounded, it wasn't really the reception I thought too much about. Instead, I thought a lot about the acknowledgements section. I knew it was going to bring me so much joy to finally be able to thank the people who made this moment happen. And trust me, I really wouldn't have had the balls or perseverance to do it without the amazing people I am surrounded by.

I've been in love with Disney since I was old enough and cognitively able to understand what I was watching. And although one would think my brother hanging off the stairs in his red underwear, pretending to be Mowgli, would be enough to put me off Disney for the rest of my life. It left mental scars, but for some unbeknownst reason, it didn't.

Yet things really kicked off back in 2016 when my cousin and her family took me to Florida. I hadn't been since I was a child. I always knew I wanted to go back, but it never seemed likely until the opportunity presented itself. From the moment we drove under the Walt Disney World signs, it became immediately apparent that I was going to be a Disney Adult.

To my cousin Beth (Dr Bob), thank you so much for reintroducing me to Walt Disney World. It scares me to think about what would've happened if we hadn't gone on that trip. I think I always would've found my way to Disney, but the mere idea of not having got that terrifies me.

You will always be my Disney partner in crime. I know for fact you and Dan are going to be on your 3rd family trip with your future kids, and of course, crazy Aunt Lydia will be in the back of the rental car, ready to fuck shit up. Whatever our Disney future holds for us, every single trip with you has been a privilege, and I wouldn't change it for the world.

Imogen, you're a fucking nob head. But you're my nob head. We've been pretty much inseparable since the day you were born, and you've stuck by me every step of the way. Even when I dressed you up in so much princess stuff, people started to get worried you would never be able to learn to walk. Maybe that's why you've always loved Ariel so much.

I quite literally couldn't have done this without you; you've been my editor, marketer, and therapist, all rolled into one. When I'd message you drunk, having second thoughts about doing this, you would tell me to shut the fuck up and get on with it. Which is precisely what I needed to hear.

I keep saying you're the Roy to my Walt, and the further we've gone down this journey, the more I've realised how important Roy was to the Disney company. Because this book wouldn't exist without you. You've got a bright future ahead of you, girl, and I can't wait to see you shine. Whatever chapter comes next, one of my favourite things about my life is having you a part of it. (Also, your boyfriend is fit. Love you Charles x)

Jamie, now you're my partner in real crime. Meeting you made me believe in soul sisters. The fact that I've even said that makes me want to vom, but this is the soppy side you bring out of me. You've never not encouraged me to strive for more. Anytime I'm scared of taking a leap, you're there to slap me around the face and push me off. Everyone needs a Jamie in their

157

fe. I hope we're arguing at 4 am about whether Disneyland would work in the UK, absolutely wrecked, for the rest of our lives.

These three girls were the first people I told about this book, and they've been there, shouting me on every step of the way. I am so grateful to you all, not just for what you've done for this book but for what you've done for my life. Florida Four forever.

This whole idea came from a blog I ran on the group called It's Orlando Time. Never in a million years did I think anyone would give a fuck what I had to say, but the response we got was nothing short of amazing. Although I have always aspired to be a writer, I've found it hard to admit that out loud.

I think I've always been scared that if I say it into the universe and then I get a bad reaction to my writing, it would ruin me, and writing is such a huge part of who I am. Those blogs were the first time I had ever properly shared my writing publicly, so to have received a positive response completely changed me.

It was through these blogs that I met Ellis J. Stewart, a brilliant author. Ellis reached out and told me that I should write a book. This was the first time I had ever had any feedback from a professional, and I was absolutely beside myself. Ellis was kind enough to provide me with a lot of advice and encouragement. I cannot thank you enough for the time you took to speak to me and for reaching out in the first place. Without your comment, I don't think I would've even thought of trying to get here.

To the people and admin of It's Orlando Time. Thank you so fucking much. It all started out as a silly little blog about constipation and bumholes, and now we're here. Thank you to everyone who took the time to comment and reach out from the blogs. Your words of encouragement completely transformed my self-esteem. Before the original blogs in 2022, I would never have had the courage to share this book.

Thank you to the admins for creating such a wonderful Disney space. When I speak about the Disney community in this book and how amazing it is, so much of that comes from you guys. The world is bat shit crazy, so to have a safe place full of such amazing people isn't taken for granted.

I can't believe it's been over two years since the first blog and here we are. It makes me very excited about what the future will bring, and I can't wait to take my IOT crew with me. I don't care whether you want to or not. I'm fucking dragging you with me.

To the team at Happy Place Print, how you got this brilliant front cover from my hilarious pencil drawing is nothing short of wizardry. Having you on board and being so excited about this book made a scary journey a little less petrifying. I have absolutely loved working with you and am obsessed with your work.

Aaron H Goldberg, author of 'The Wonders of Walt Disney World.' Thank you for being so rational when I was absolutely spiralling about this book. You motivated me to get back on the horse, and again, I don't know if I would've made it here without your kindness.

Ok I've got to bring more of my family into this, or Christmas is going to be unbearable for me. To my Mum & Dean, thank you for listening to me ramble on after a couple of bottles of wine about my crazy goals and ambitions. Thank you for always being there for me and supporting me regardless of how mental I am. Dean, I'll force you into Walt Disney World one day, and whether it is the worst trip of your life or the best, I'm going to find it wildly entertaining.

Dad, thank you for always having my back. For being my voice f reason and forever answering my Dad questions. Jack, you o my fucking head in, but I love you to bits.

To all my grandparents, your support changed everything or me. It will always bother me that grandchildren get limited ime with their grandparents; I want to be 70 and still be able o go around to my grandparents (Jill & Pete) for their 10/10 nack selection. I'm very lucky to have them in my life still, and cherish all the time I spend with them. No matter how dark ny days are, they find a way to brighten it up.

Pops, thank you for never giving up on me. No one has fought arder for me, and I will forever be grateful for that.

Charlie and Shannon, life would undoubtedly be a lot duller vithout you guys in it. You're some of my biggest cheerleaders, nd I love you for it. Theresa, Emily, Kristie & Kate, my OGs, ou guys know more than anyone how long I've been chatting hit about writing a book. Thank you for always rooting for ne. Phoebe (Pheebsecco), your crazy Aunt Lydia is going to orce you to love Disney whether you like it or not. If you don't, you're going to have to get very good at pretending.

To all the creatives, past and present, at Disney, thank you or being such a massive part of my life. Disney is the reason I ell in love with storytelling and why I am so passionate about my future as a filmmaker. Thank you for giving so much of yourselves to this industry and creating stories that have quite iterally changed my life. I have so much love and admiration for everyone at the Disney company. And if you send Mickey after me, so be it.

Nia, thank you for being my Disney work wife. Your excitement for this book reignited a passion in me to keep going with it. To the other amazing people in my industry who have driven me, inspired me and given me opportunities: Fay, Eden,

Cristiane, Peace, Raven T, Raven MT. I appreciate you.

I could honestly keep going, but before I start thanking m
neighbour's sister's friend's cat, I'm going to wrap this up. A
you can tell, I really didn't do this alone. So many people hav
been on this journey with me, and I owe them so much.

If you've read this book and made it this far, you're probabl
who I need to thank the most. As I write this, it still feels s
surreal that someone might choose to read my book from star
to finish. So, whoever is holding this book in hand right now
thank you. Thank you, thank you, THANK YOU! I probabl
shouldn't admit as an aspiring writer that I'm struggling t
find words, but I'm not sure I'll ever be able to find ones tha
truly emphasise how fucking grateful I am that you're reading
this. Which probably is a relief. I think I've chatted enough
shite for now.

It felt like I was never going to finish this book. I just kep
going back and adding and removing and panicking. I was
plussing the fuck out of it. I knew there had to come a point
where I had to say enough. Otherwise, I'd be rewriting this book
into my retirement.

I finally accepted that I was going to make mistakes and that
there were going to be things I would wish I had done differently
This is mine and Imogen's first time doing this, and we've done
our absolute best—grammar errors and all! I had to accept that
and know that whatever I learnt from my mistakes with this
project, I would apply it to my next one. I never, ever want to
stop working on myself as a creative. Walt taught me that.

Whatever happens, whatever is in store for me next and in
the future, bring it on. Because it's never goodbye; it's always:
Stay tuned.

Much love, your favourite fucked-up Disney Adult - Lyds xo

Bibliography

Don't you dare fucking judge how many Wikipedia links are here.

"A Legacy of Leaders: Disney CEOs Through the Years." *World of Walt*, 5 Mar. 2020, worldofwalt.com/a-legacy-of-leaders-disney-ceos-through-the-years.html.

"A Look Back at Early Walt Disney World Merchandising." *Disney Parks Blog*, disneyparks.disney.go.com/blog/2011/09/a-look-back-at-early-walt-disney-world-resort-merchandise/.

"Academy Awards Won by Walt Disney Pictures." *Disney Fandom*, disney.fandom.com/wiki/Academy_Awards_won_by_Walt_Dis-ney_Pictures

"Animal Kingdom." *Wikipedia*, Wikimedia Foundation, 7 Sept. 2024, en.wikipedia.org/wiki/Disney%27s_Animal_Kingdom.

"Birth of Mickey Mouse." *Maya Academy of Advanced Creativity*, www.maacindia.com/blog/birth-of-mickey-mouse/.

"Caring for Our Cast." *Disney Experiences*, disneycon-nect.com/disney-aspire/.

"Delivering Joy When It's Needed Most." *The Walt Disney Company*, impact.disney.com/charitable-giving/childrens hospitals-wish-granting/.

"Disney Adult Internet Culture." *In Style*, www.instyle.com/disney-adult-internet-culture-6741302.

"Disney Adult." *Urban* Dictionary, January 28 2021. https://www.urbandictionary.com/define.php?term=Disney%20Adult

"Disney Adults." *Wikipedia*, Wikimedia Foundation, 25 Aug. 2024, en.wikipedia.org/wiki/Disney_adult.

"Disney Cruise Line." *Wikipedia*, Wikimedia Foundation, 27 Aug. 2024, en.wikipedia.org/wiki/Disney_Cruise_Line.

"Disney History." *D23.* https://d23.com/disney-history/

"Disney World Grand Opening." *This Day in Disney History*, www.thisdayindisneyhistory.com/WorldOfDisneyParks.html.

"Disneyana." *Wikipedia*, Wikimedia Foundation, 27 May 2023,

"History of Mickey Mouse Ears." *Mickey Mouse Ears*, www.mickeymouseears.com/history-of-mickey-mouse-ears.html.

"Honouring the Heart of Our Magic." *Disney Parks Blog*, disneyparks.disney.go.com/blog/2021/09/honoring-the-heart-of-our-magic-cast-members-of-past-present-and-future/.

"How Disney's Animal Kingdom Became a Beacon of Conservation." *The Walt Disney Company*, 21 Apr. 2023, thewaltdisneycompany.com/how-disneys-animal-kingdom-became-a-beacon-of-conservation/.

"How to Do the Disney D23 Expo with Kids." *Little Gray Thread*, 27 Aug. 2019, littlegraythread.wordpress.com/2019/08/27/how-to-do-the-disney-d23-expo-with-kids/.

"InWalt'sOwnWords:AdultsSeeingDisneyFilms."*WalDisney*, www.waltdisney.org/blog/walts-own-words-adults-seeing-disney-films.

"It's Orlando Time." *Facebook*, www.facebook.com/groups/OR-LANDOTIME/?locale=en_GB.

"List of Disney Films." *D23*. https://d23.com/list-of-disney-films/
 "Mickey Mouse." *Wikipedia*, Wikimedia Foundation, 10 Sept. 2024, en.wikipedia.org/wiki/Mickey_Mouse.

"Mr. Toad's Pals Protest to Disney World." *St. Louis Post-Dispatch*, 6 Sept. 1998, p. 23.

"Oswald the Lucky Rabbit." *Wikipedia*, Wikimedia Foundation, 15 Sept. 2024, en.wikipedia.org/wiki/Oswald_the_Lucky_Rab-bit.

"Our Story." *Pixar*, www.pixar.com/our-story.

"Overview of Disney World's Disability Access Service (DAS)."*Undercover Tourist*, 4 Jul. 2024, www.undercover-tourist.com/blog/disability-access-das-card/.

"Reinventing the American Amusement Park." *American Experi-ence*, www.pbs.org/wgbh/americanexperience/ features/reinventing-american-amusement-park/.

"The Dapper Day Story." *Dapper Day*, dapperday.com/pages/ the-dapper-day-story.

"The Ins and Outs of Disney World's Advance Dining Reservation System." *Undercover Tourist*, www.under-covertourist.com/blog/ins-outs-disneys-advance-dining-reservation-system/#.

"The Pyramid in Practice – It All Begins with a Story and Frozen Ever After." *The Imagineering Toolbox*, 29 Jun 2016, imagineeringtoolbox.wordpress.com/2016/06/29/ the-pyramid-in-practice-it-all-begins-with-a-story-and-
frozen-ever-after/.

"Thousands Line Up for Figment Popcorn Bucket at EPCOT." *Blog Mickey*, 14 Jan. 2022, blogmickey.com/2022/01/thousands-line-up-for-figment-popcorn-bucket-at-epcot/.

"Timeline of the Walt Disney Company." *Wikipedia*, Wikimedia Foundation, September 7 2024. https://en.wikipedia.org/wiki/ Timeline_of_the_Walt_Disney_Company

"Walt Disney's FAVORITE Animated Moment." *YouTube*, up-loaded by Sean Dudley, 16 Jan. 2023, www.youtube.com/ watch?v=PN-

Qeq Ae1OWo

"WDW 50 – Dedication Ceremony for Cast Member Plaque Held at Magic Kingdom." *Laughing Place*, 16 Dec. 2021, www.laughingplace.com/w/news/2021/09/16/cast-member-plaque-dedication-ceremony-magic-kingdom/.

"World of Disney Parks." *This Day in Disney History*, www.thisdayindisneyhistory.com/WorldOfDisneyParks.html.

Adventures By Disney, www.adventuresbydisney.com.

Albert, S. "How to Thank Disney World Cast Members." *WDW Prep School*, 31 Jan. 2014, wdwprepschool.com/how-to-thank-disney-world-cast-members/.

Baker, J. "Disney Theme Parks: The History and the Magic." *Life*, 15 Jul. 2024, www.life.com/destinations/disney-theme-parks-the-history-and-the-magic/.

Brooman,S."Dad's Disneyland Selfie Goes Viral After He Crops Out Daughter From Photo."*Diply*,diply.com/dads-disneyland-selfie-goes-viral-after-he-crops-out-daughter-f/.

Bugden, R. "A Short History of Disney Merchandising." *Medium*, 3 May 2019, medium.com/the-wonderful-world-of-disney/a-short-history-of-disney-merchandising-b9441a94 bbb4

Cash, M. "A mom's Facebook post that 'childless millennials' shouldn't be allowed at Disney parks is wrong and sexist." *Business Insider,* July 30 2019. https://www.businessinsider.

com/moms-rant-that-disney-should-ban-childless-millenn
ials-is-sexist-2019-7

Catmull, E, and A Wallace. *Creativity, Inc. (The Expanded Edition): Overcoming the Unseen Forces That Stand in the Way of True Inspiration. Random House LLC US*, 2023.

D23. https://d23.com/about-the-expo/

D23. https://d23.com/about-walt-disney/

Davis, C. "Will Disney Ever Win Best Picture? 'West Side Story" Is Another Loophole Chance.' *Variety,* January 6 2022. https://variety.com/2022/awards/awards/disney-oscars-best-picture-encanto-spider-man-avatar-1235147493/

Determan, S. 'The many merry eras of Disney.' *BFI*, February 18 2021. https://www.bfi.org.uk/features/many-merry-eras-disney

Dickson, E. "How 'Disney Adults' Became the Most Hated Group on the Internet." *Rolling Stone*, June 21 2022. https://www.rollingstone.com/culture/culture-features/disney-adults-tiktok-hated-internet-1370226/

Disneyana Fan Club, disneyanafanclub.weebly.com.

Eisenberg, Eric. "Frozen Is The New Title For Disney's Snow Queen Movie, Not Pixar's Dinosaur Project." *Cinema Blend*, 22 Dec. 2011, www.cinemablend.com/new/Frozen-Title-Disney-Snow-Queen-Movie-Pixar-Dinosaur-Project-28499.html.

Fantozzi, J, and V Montalti . "27 Secrets Every Disney World Lover Should Know." *Business Insider*, 7 Mar. 2022, www.insider.com/disney-world-secrets-facts-2018-1#there-is-a-secret-suite-inside-cinderella-castle-thats-only-open-to-contest-winners-and-special-guests-3.

Franco, M. "The 10 Most Lucrative Movie Merchandise Franchises, from 'Star Wars' and 'Batman' to 'Frozen'and 'Cars'." *Indie Wire*, 6 Aug. 2023, www.indiewire.com/gallery/movies-that-sold-the-most-merchandise-star-wars-frozen-batman/msdbatm-wb003/.

Franklin, MA. *Following the Mouse: A Historical and Cultural Analysis of the Disney Fan Community.* 2012. California State University,Northridge, Master of Arts in Sociology.

French, S. "The Guide to Disney Vacation Club." *Nerd Wallet*, 11 Sept. 2024, www.nerdwallet.com/article/travel/disney-vacation-club.

Fresen, N. "Primark UnveilsNew Collection Celebrating 100 Years of Disney." *Business Insider*, 17 Feb. 2023, www.theretailbulletin.com/fashion/primark-unveils-new-collection-celebrating-100-years-of-disney-17-02-2023/

GoldenOakRealty, www.disneygoldenoak.com.

Heinrich, S. This Couple Decided To Forgo At Their Wedding So Minnie AndMickeyCouldMakeAnAppearance,AndIt'sSparking ADiscussionAbout"DisneyAdults"*BuzzFeed*,June72022.https://www.buzzfeed.com/shelbyheinrich/disne

y-wedding-reddit-aita

Iger, R. *The Ride of a Lifetime: Lessons in Creative Leadership from 15 Years As CEO of the Walt Disney Company. Bantam Press*, 2019.

Kinni, T, and W Lefkon. *Be Our Guest (10th Anniversary Updated Edition): Perfecting the Art of Customer Service. Disney Editions*, 2011.

Levy, L. *To Pixar and Beyond: My Unlikely Journey with Steve Jobs to Make Entertainment History. Oneworld Publications*, 2017.

Liberatore, S. "The Science behind 'Disney Adults': Experts Reveal Why Some People Are Obsessed with 'the Happiest Place on Earth'." *Daily Mail*, 10 Oct. 2023, www.daily-mail.co.uk/sciencetech/article-12616113/science-disney-adults-experts.html#:~:text=These%20so%2Dcalled%20Disney%20adults,or%20a%20sense%20of%20belonging.

Lipp, D. *Disney U: How Disney University Develops the World's Most Engaged, Loyal, and Customer-Centric Employees. McGraw Hill*, 2013.

Oliveros, K. "The 10 Most Lucrative Movie Merchandise Franchises, from 'Star Wars' and 'Batman' to 'Frozen' and 'Cars'." *Disney Food Blog*, www.disneyfoodblog.com/2021/10/01/the-longest-lines-youll-wait-in-today-wont-be-for-disney-worlds-rides/.

Palmer, T. "Rich Manhattan Moms Hire Handicapped Tour Guides so Kids Can Cut Lines at Disney World." *New York Post*,

14 May 2013, nypost.com/2013/05/14/rich-manhattan-moms-hire-handicapped-tour-guides-so-kids-can-cut-lines-at-disney-world/.

Piccuito, E. "Disney World Means Everything to a Special Needs Mom." *Daily Beast*, 14 Apr. 2017, www.thedaily-beast.com/disney-world-means-everything-to-a-special-needs-mom.

Rapp, J. "5 Things You Need to Know About the Blue Legacy Name Tag." *Disney Parks Blog*, 7 Mar. 2022, disneyparks.disney.go.com/blog/2022/03/5-things-you-need-to-know-about-the-blue-legacy-name-tag/.

Rhodes, Elizabeth. "Looking Back at Disneyland's Opening Day, Almost 70 Years Later." *Travel & Leisure*, 15 Jul. 2024, www.trav-elandleisure.com/trip-ideas/disney-vacations/disneyland-anniversary-65-years.

Sim, N. "5 Ways Disney Cast Members Go Above and Beyond for Guests Every Day." *Theme Park Tourist*, www.themepark-tourist.com/5-ways-disney-cast-members-go-above-and-beyond-guests-every-day/.

Smith, H. "Why Are Disney Employees Called Cast Members? Here'S Why." *Florida Parks*, 4 Aug. 2023, orlando-deals.co.uk/blog/why-are-disney-employees-called-cast-members/.

Story Living by Disney, www.storylivingbydisney.com.

Terzigni, C. "Everything You've EVER Wanted to Know About the History of Disney's Dole Whip!" *Disney Food Blog*, www.disneyfoodblog.com/2020/06/14/everything-youve-ever-wanted-to-know-about-the-history-of-disneys-dole-whip/.

Tyler, A, and S Lela's. "Every Pixar Movie Easter Egg That Teased A Future Film." *Screen Rant*, 25 Jun. 2024, screenrant.com/pixar-movies-easter-eggs-future-film-teases-hints/.

Williams, L. "Disney Adults Might Be Onto Something." *Bustle*, 14 Jun. 2023, www.bustle.com/life/disney-adults-psychology.

Williams, P. *How to Be Like Walt: Capturing the Disney Magic Every Day of Your Life. Health Communications Inc*, 2004.

Yossman, KJ. "Confessions of Disney Adults: Mouse House Superfans Talk Splurging on Merch, Keeping Execs in Check." *Variety*, 16 Oct. 2023, variety.com/2023/biz/global/confessions-of-disney-adults-disneyland-world-merchandise-bob-iger-1235757415/.

STEINER STORIES

Printed in Great Britain
by Amazon

53047734R00126